Stupid History

Other Books by Leland Gregory

What's the Number for 911?

What's the Number for 911 Again?

The Stupid Crook Book

Hey, Idiot!

Idiots at Work

Bush-Whacked

Idiots in Love

Am-Bushed!

Stupid History

Idiots in Charge

Cruel and Unusual Idiots

What's the Number for 911?: Second Edition

Stupid History

A Collection of Stupidity, Strangeness, and Mythconceptions Through the Ages

Leland Gregory

**Andrews McMeel
Publishing**®

Kansas City • Sydney • London

Andrews McMeel Publishing, LLC
an Andrews McMeel Universal company
1130 Walnut Street, Kansas City, Missouri 64106

www.andrewsmcmeel.com

14 15 16 17 18 RR2 10 9 8 7 6 5 4 3 2 1

ISBN: 978-1-4494-5713-6

Book design by Holly Camerlinck
Illustrations by Kevin Brimmer

Attention: Schools and Businesses

Andrews McMeel books are available at quantity discounts with
bulk purchase for educational, business, or sales promotional use.
For information, please e-mail the Andrews McMeel Publishing
Special Sales Department: specialsales@amuniversal.com

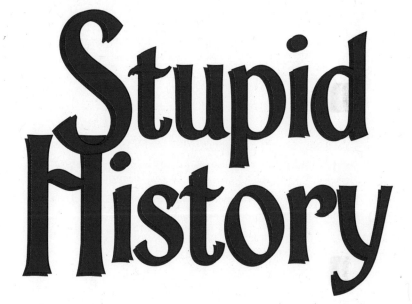

Why Is Paul Revere Revered?

"Listen, my children, and you shall hear
Of the midnight ride of Paul Revere..."

"The Landlord's Tale: Paul Revere's Ride" by Henry Wadsworth Longfellow (not "The Midnight Ride of Paul Revere," as most people call it) is one of the best-known poems in American historical literature. But it's a poem—it isn't actual history. Paul Revere didn't make the historical ride into Concord, Massachusetts, to warn the citizens "the British are coming!" He did, however, ride into Lexington on April 17, 1775, warning "the regulars are coming!" (The British army was referred to as the "regular troops.") On April 18, Paul Revere, a cobbler named William Dawes, and a doctor named Samuel Prescott were heading toward Concord to warn the citizens about British troop movements. Unfortunately, the three were spotted by a British patrol, and Revere was captured and detained. Dawes headed back toward Lexington, but Prescott continued on into Concord and was able to warn the citizens. Revere was released by the British the next day and had to return to Lexington on foot—they'd kept his horse. So actually, it was a doctor named Samuel Prescott who made the immortal ride into Concord, not Revere. I suppose Longfellow chose Revere because it's easier to rhyme than Prescott.

The Myth of Magellan

After learning about Christopher Columbus sailing the ocean blue in 1492, we were taught that Ferdinand Magellan sailed around the world in a single trip (or *circumnavigated* the globe, if you will). Well, he didn't. Magellan, a Portuguese captain in the service of Spain, set out on August 10, 1519, from Seville with five ships and a crew of 250 men. Things didn't go so well for old Magellan, though. His three-year journey was plagued with terrible weather, maps that weren't up to date, starvation, and a violent mutiny. The truth of the matter is only one of Magellan's ships, the *Victoria*, arrived back at Seville, with only eighteen of its fifty crewmembers alive. One other person who didn't make it was Ferdinand Magellan himself. When his ship landed on Mactan Island in the Philippines, he was met with a less than friendly reception party. Magellan died, face down on the beach, looking like a pincushion from the numerous spears sticking out of his body.

Buttermilk does not contain butter. It is a
by-product of the butter-making process and
contains less fat than whole milk.

C lement Clarke Moore's famous poem is not called "'Twas the Night Before Christmas," but is actually titled "A Visit from Saint Nicholas." The sugarplums mentioned in the poem (and seen in Tchaikovsky's *Nutcracker Suite*) have nothing to do with plums. They are actually hard candies.

Taking a Whack at the Truth

A lot of erroneous history is passed down in books, plays, movies, and poems—usually these were intended to be entertainment, not historical truths. But some of these false facts are so ingrained in our consciousness that there's little chance of the truth becoming as popular as the fiction. Here's an example: What do you think of when you hear the name Lizzie Borden? Everyone chant with me:

> "Lizzie Borden took an ax
> And gave her mother forty whacks.
> When she saw what she had done
> She gave her father forty-one."

Since she was first suspected of hacking her parents to death in 1892, Lizzie Borden has stood out as one of the few female homicidal maniacs in history—and if it wasn't for this little refrain, her name would have been forgotten years ago. What is forgotten is that a jury acquitted Lizzie Borden after only sixty-six minutes of deliberation and all charges were dropped. I hope the truth about Lizzie's innocence becomes as popular as the song—and then we can all just bury the hatchet.

Benjamin Franklin Didn't Discover Electricity? What a Shock!

Here's the quickest way to disprove that Benjamin Franklin discovered electricity—it already had a name. *Electricity* comes from the Greek word *elektron*, which means "amber." (The Greeks discovered they could generate static electricity by rubbing amber with fur.) What Franklin was trying to prove in his 1752 experiment was the electrical nature of lightning—that lightning was, in fact, electricity. It is true that Franklin flew a kite with a key tied to the string—but the kite was not struck by lightning. If it had been, Franklin might have become a has-Ben. The spark that leapt from the key to Franklin's knuckle was caused by the flow of electrons that exists at all times between the ground and the sky—but during a thunderstorm, the electrons are more active. Had Benjamin Franklin, the inventor of bifocal glasses, actually been struck by lightning, he would have made a real spectacle of himself.

❦

Horseshoe crabs are not crabs. They are survivors
of a species that became extinct 175 million years ago.
Their closest modern relatives are scorpions and spiders.

Return to Sender—
Address Unknown

Abraham Lincoln's Gettysburg Address is considered one of the most moving and brilliantly written speeches of all time. And the most fascinating aspect of the speech is that Lincoln wrote it on the back of an envelope while traveling by train through Pennsylvania. Wrong! It would be wonderful to believe this masterpiece was so divinely inspired that Lincoln dashed it off in a matter of minutes. But the truth is, Lincoln began working on the Gettysburg Address eleven days before he gave the speech on November 19, 1863. In fact, there are five drafts of the speech still in existence—some even written on White House stationery. Maybe because the speech is fewer than 300 words, people have assumed he just pulled it out of his hat.

By Any Means Necessary

Here's another well-known fact about President Abraham Lincoln: The Emancipation Proclamation freed the slaves, right? Well, no. The Proclamation, issued by Lincoln on January 1, 1863, proposed freeing slaves in the Southern states only—it didn't mention ending slavery in the North. Even Lincoln's secretary of state, William Henry Seward, saw the irony in this and stated, "We show our sympathy with slavery by emancipating slaves where we cannot reach them and holding them in bondage where we can set them free."

Before he issued the Emancipation Proclamation, Lincoln threatened the South by saying if they didn't rejoin the Union, he would abolish slavery. They didn't, and he had to follow through with his threat—but it was an empty threat because the South had already seceded and Lincoln had no authority over it. Lincoln's real reason for the Proclamation was made very clear in a letter he sent to the *New York Times*:

> My paramount objective in this struggle is to save the Union, and is not to save or destroy slavery. If I could save the Union without freeing any slaves, I would do it, and if I could save it by freeing all slaves, I would do it; and if I could save it by freeing some and leaving others alone, I would do that.

Although we are all taught that Lincoln's Emancipation Proclamation freed the slaves, it didn't. What did free the slaves was the 13th Amendment to the Constitution, which was ratified in the latter part of 1865—and unfortunately, Lincoln was dead by that time.

The Color Is Plane Wrong

Even though the flight data recorder carried on all military and commercial planes is called a "black box," it is, in fact, bright orange. It wouldn't make sense to paint the box black, as that would only make it harder to find after a plane wreck.

❧

Despite their name, centipedes do not necessarily
have 100 legs; the number of appendages ranges anywhere
from 28 to 354, depending on the species.
And millipedes don't have a thousand legs, either.

The Lightbulb Was Not Edison's Bright Idea

Thomas Alva Edison is credited with hundreds of inventions; not the least of these is the electric lightbulb. Ask any schoolchild who invented the lightbulb, and he or she will, without hesitation, name Thomas Edison. But the truly illuminated know the first lightbulb was actually invented in 1802 (nearly seventy-seven years before Edison's version) by an English chemist, Sir Humphry Davy, who made an arc lamp glow by passing electricity through a platinum wire. Davy never pursued any practical use for his invention, and the world stayed dependent on candlepower and oil lamps for several more decades. In 1845, an American, J. W. Starr, developed a lightbulb using a vacuum bulb and a carbon filament—a design very similar to Edison's. When Starr died at the age of twenty-five, an Englishman, Sir Joseph Wilson Swan, continued to work on his design. The main problem with this and previous designs was that the filament would burn only for a short while, rendering the lightbulb impractical for any real use. In 1877, Edison went about searching for a filament that could stay illuminated for a long period of time. After trying nearly 8,000 possibilities, he found

one—a carbonized cotton thread. So Edison discovered a way to make a lightbulb work for an extended period of time? Not really. Remember Joseph Swan? Well, he discovered using a carbonized piece of cotton thread would do the trick, too—ten months earlier. In fact, he filed a patent infringement suit against Edison and won. So Edison, living up to his credo that "genius is one percent inspiration and ninety-nine percent perspiration" became inspired, made Swan a partner in his lighting company, and later bought him out.

Captains Cannot Tie Knots

The captain of a ship is usually known for two things: volunteering to go down with a sinking ship and performing marriages. Well, we all know the first one isn't always true, as countless captains have returned safe and sound after disasters on the high seas. But the second one, that of a captain being able to perform a wedding ceremony, is also false. The case of *Norman v. Norman* in 1898 established that the captain of a ship has never had any legal authority to perform a wedding.

George Washington could never have thrown a silver dollar across the Potomac River. The first dollar coin was minted in 1794, just five years before Washington's death. Also, the Potomac is over a half-mile wide at its narrowest point.

The Evening Star Is a Stand-In

Shortly after sunset, one can see a bright beacon of light called the Evening Star over the western horizon. There's no use wishing on this star, as it is an impostor—it's actually the planet Venus.

Corn oil is derived from corn, so banana oil must come from bananas. Actually, banana oil is a petroleum chemical used in lacquers and glues that has a faint banana scent.

Real Steamboat Inventor Steamed

Robert Fulton is usually credited with inventing the steamboat in 1807, and the name of his boat is given as the *Clermont*. But as you'll find from most of the entries in this book, like steam, most of what we know about history is full of hot air. A man named James Rumsey exhibited a crude steamboat on the Potomac in 1784, and three years later, John Fitch demonstrated a forty-five-foot steamboat to the Continental Congress.

Fitch tried to establish a regular passenger service between Philadelphia and New Jersey, but his venture ran out of steam. So why does Robert Fulton get all the glory and not the men who truly invented the steamboat? Because Fulton established a successful steamboat line on the Hudson River between New York and Albany, and we usually remember people who become popular. Fulton's boat was called *North River Steamboat*, but because the town of Clermont was the first port on its route, it acquired the nickname *Clermont*. John Fitch, who was granted the patent on the steamboat in 1791, died broke, while Fulton drove full steam ahead into our history books.

The Great Wall of China Is Out of Sight

Part of the mystique surrounding this amazing engineering marvel is that the 1,864-mile-long wall of China can be seen from space. But when one actually stops to think about this claim, it simply crumbles. Why would the Great Wall be seen from space when Beijing's new Golden Resources Shopping Mall, the world's largest at six million square feet, can't be? The foundation for the wall story started in 1938, when Richard Halliburton, in his book *Second Book of Marvels*, announced that the Great Wall is the only man-made object visible from the moon. I suppose a sequel to this book would include how Halliburton could know that, when it would be another thirty-one years before *Apollo 11* actually landed on the moon. And according to the astronauts, not even the earth's largest mountain ranges are visible from the moon.

One Half of All Marriages End in Divorce

This statistic is the ace in the hole when it comes to showing the moral decay of our times—politicians use it, preachers use it, marriage counselors use it—but statistically speaking, it's useless. This figure is derived by taking the number of marriages per year and comparing it to the number of divorces per year. And since there are nearly half as many divorces as marriages, people conclude that half of all marriages end in divorce. This statistic would be correct if everyone married only once and divorced only once, but thanks to the Larry Kings and Elizabeth Taylors of the world, things just don't add up. The actual number of marriages that end in divorce is closer to 1 in 4, or 25 percent.

Even though people still believe you can get lead poisoning from a pencil, you can't. Lead pencils have no lead in them, only graphite.

His Name Wasn't Schicklgruber, Either

Adolf Hitler was neither a housepainter nor a wallpaper-hanger before he became ruler of Germany. He was a moderately talented watercolor artist but flunked the drawing tests at the Vienna Academy of Fine Arts and was told his talents were better suited to architecture. In turn, he became the architect of the Third Reich and was responsible for one of the darkest periods in world history.

Philadelphia Brand cream cheese was not originally manufactured in the City of Brotherly Love, but rather in the Big Apple, New York. The cream cheese was branded Philadelphia to take advantage of the reputation for fine food the city had at the time.

The Truth of William Tell Told

It's a disturbing story, to say the least. An oppressive bailiff named Hermann Gessler was sent from Austria to Switzerland in the early 1300s to maintain control of the people. He placed his hat on a pole and ordered the citizens to salute or bow to the hat to show their allegiance. William Tell, along with his son Walter, walked by the hat without honoring it and were accosted by guards. Gessler forced William Tell to shoot an apple off his son's head in exchange for his freedom. Tell put one arrow in his crossbow and another in his quiver and easily shot the apple from his son's head. When asked what the other arrow was for, Tell told Gessler if he had hurt his son during the stunt, he would have used the extra arrow to kill Gessler. Needless to say, Gessler got the point. He was infuriated by Tell's arrogance and ordered him imprisoned for the rest of his life.

Tell's legendary prowess with the crossbow and unfailing love of freedom made him the hero of Swiss independence. The story would be even more disturbing if it were true, but it isn't. William Tell didn't have a son, didn't own a crossbow, and never even saw an apple. Why? Because William Tell never existed. The great fourteenth-century hero of Swiss independence was born in the imagination of an anonymous fifteenth-century storyteller. I quiver when I think how many people have been shafted into believing this story is real.

Ladies and Gentlemen, the Beetles!

In 1545, an angry crowd of vineyard growers in Saint-Julien, France, pleaded with a judge to throw the book at local pests who were eating and destroying their crops—weevils. Believe it or not, the judge ordered legal indictments to be drawn, and the weevils were given a court-appointed defense lawyer (and the lawyer/vermin relationship was born).

The judge listened to both sides and eventually passed judgment, finding the weevils guilty, since they were obviously eating the crops. In 1546, the judge issued a proclamation demanding the weevils cease and desist. Being the law-abiding insects they were, the weevils did stop eating the crops, and their infestation disappeared nearly overnight. The weevils didn't bug anyone for forty years, until 1587, when they once again took residence in the vineyards of Saint-Julien, and once again, the angry growers took the pests to court. There's no record of whether the court threw the book at the weevils again or merely used it to squish them.

In 1716, the Oxford University Press printed 500 copies of a book titled *Translation of the New Testament from Coptic into Latin*, by David Wilkins. Not exactly a John Grisham novel, it took 191 years to sell all 500 copies.

Stop Clowning Around

The *Kansas City Star* ran a blurb about National Clown Week on its July 30, 1999, "Family Fun" page. Naturally, the editorial decision was made to include a silly, funny picture of a clown to accompany the article. How could you go wrong putting a picture of an adorable, goofy clown in your newspaper? Well, the only way would be if the clown in question was actually notorious serial killer John Wayne Gacy. Besides being a convicted murderer of thirty-three boys and young men, Gacy, a Chicago native, was also an amateur clown who went by the name of "Pogo the Clown." It was a picture of Gacy in clown makeup that was used alongside the article about National Clown Week. The *Star* printed an editor's note the following day apologizing for being such Bozos.

The headline from a *Los Angeles Times* article in 1972 read "70-Car Fog Pileup." In truth, only sixty-nine cars, not seventy, were involved in the accident, but an editor thought sixty-nine was a dirty number.

Bringing Down the House

The world's first fireproof theater, the Iroquois Theater, opened in Chicago on December 1, 1903. This was a big deal for Chicago, because in 1871, the city nearly burned to the ground, and no one wanted that to happen again.

On December 30, it was standing room only, as 1,900 people packed the theater to watch the popular musical *Mr. Blue Beard, Jr.* As the audience listened to a close harmony version of "In the Pale Moonlight," a blue stage light used to create a moonglow effect popped, and a piece of scenery caught on fire. "Not to worry," the actors told the audience, "please remain seated as we lower the asbestos curtain."

The secure feeling of being in a fireproof theater was quickly doused when the safety curtain jammed two thirds of the way down. The titanic claims of indestructibility turned the first fireproof theater into Chicago's deadliest fire in history. The Iroquois Theater, the toast of Chicago, was now toast.

As a member of Parliament, Sir Isaac Newton spoke only once. He asked for an open window.

There's a Hole in the Bottom of the Sea

Lake Peigneur, a scenic lake near New Iberia, Louisiana, was home to Jefferson Island and the beautiful Live Oak Gardens botanical park. In stark contrast to the natural beauty were the numerous oil and gas rigs that dotted the landscape. On the morning of November 21, 1980, Wilson Brothers Corporation, which had been hired by Texaco to tap into Louisiana's rich oil deposits, set up an oil rig in the middle of Lake Peigneur and started drilling. A test hole was being drilled at Well No. 20, and things were going along normally until the drill hit 1,228 feet. Instead of the classic scene of oil shooting up into the air, the engineers noticed that a whirlpool had formed, and the 1,300-acre lake was quickly disappearing. The crew had inadvertently drilled into the Diamond Crystal salt mine, and the lake water was pouring into the tunnels. They watched dumbfounded as their five-million-dollar rig, a tugboat, eleven barges from the canal, a barge loading dock, seventy acres of Jefferson Island and its botanical gardens, parts of greenhouses, a house trailer, trucks, tractors, a parking lot, and a whole lot of other stuff went down the drain. Fortunately, one thing that didn't go down the drain was Leone Viator Jr. and his nephew, Timmy, who were fishing off a fourteen-foot aluminum boat when the disaster struck. The water drained so quickly their boat got stuck in the mud at the bottom of the lake, and they were able to walk back to shore. It's rare that a fisherman can say *he* was the one that got away.

Oh, Hell, Caesar

Claudius I (Tiberius Claudius Caesar Augustus Germanicus, 10 B.C.–A.D. 54) was poisoned by his wife, Agrippina, with a lethal dose of mushrooms. As he lay writhing on the floor, a doctor was summoned to his aid. The doctor thought if he could make the emperor throw up the noxious mushrooms, that might save Claudius's life. The doctor took a feather and began tickling the emperor's throat, hoping to stimulate the gag reflex. The responsibility of saving the ruler of the Roman Empire might have been distracting to the doctor, who lost his grip on the feather. Claudius inhaled the feather into his throat and chocked to death on it.

On April 24, 1898, Spain declared war
on the United States, thus starting
the Spanish-American War. The United
States declared war the very next day but,
not wanting to be outdone, had the date on
the declaration of war read April 21 instead
of April 25.

Not a Barrel of Laughs

In 1920, fifty-eight-year-old barber Charles Stephens wanted to take his high-dive and parachute artistry to new heights and maybe make a splash as a world-famous daredevil. So Stephens rolled out the barrel and let everyone know he was going to attempt the ultimate in stunts—going over Niagara Falls in a barrel. He thought adding extra weight to the barrel's bottom would help stabilize it, so he attached a 100-pound anvil, climbed into the barrel, strapped his feet to the anvil, surrounded himself with pillows, and placed his arms through two straps that were bolted inside. The force of the plunge tore open the bottom of the barrel, taking the anvil, with Stephens still strapped to it, to the bottom of the river. The barrel disintegrated on impact, and the only piece ever recovered was a stave with the right arm strap attached to it. How did they know it was the right arm strap? Because Stephens's right arm, with a tattoo reading "Forget me not, Annie," was still in the strap. Annie was his wife and the mother of his eleven children whom Stephens, with his Wile E. Coyote stunt, left behind and over a barrel.

Sticking His Neck Out

A large number of resolutions pass through the Texas State House every session, and Representative Tom Moore Jr. was concerned at how little attention legislators paid to the bills on which they voted. So in 1971, as a joke, he introduced a bill honoring Albert DeSalvo for his pioneering work in population control. DeSalvo, the notorious Boston Strangler, confessed to killing thirteen women in the Boston area. Moore's bill commended the Boston Strangler for serving

> *his country, his state, and his community. . . . This*
> *compassionate gentleman's dedication and devotion to his work*
> *has enabled the weak and lonely throughout the nation to achieve*
> *and maintain a new degree of concern for their future. . . . He*
> *has been officially recognized by the state of Massachusetts for*
> *his noted activities and unconventional techniques involving*
> *population control and applied psychology.*

The resolution passed unanimously. I'm sure Representative Moore could barely choke back his laughter.

The letter *D* in D-Day has given rise to many assumptions of its meaning: Dooms-Day, Death-Day, Deliverance-Day, etc. But the truth is the *D* stands for "Day" in the same manner the *H* in H-Hour stands for "Hour."

King for a Day

In a bizarre quirk in American history, we actually had a president who served for only one day, and his name was David Rice Atchison. James K. Polk's term ended at noon on March 4, 1849, and Zachary Taylor was scheduled to take the presidential oath of office that same day. But March 4 fell on a Sunday, and Taylor decided to take the oath on Monday instead. That meant from noon on March 4, when Polk's term expired, until noon of March 5, when Taylor was sworn in, the United States was without a president. The Constitution states: "In case of the removal, death, resignation or disability of both the President and Vice President of the United States, the President of the Senate Pro Tempore shall act as President." The president of the Senate pro tempore at the time was—you got it—David Rice Atchison. Atchison was never sworn in, never lived at the White House, and didn't know he had been president for a day until years later. He has been denied his place among the other presidents of the United States—which is just as well, since people are generally known by the company they keep.

A Real Shoe-In

In the 1600s, Louis XIV of France (born 1638, ruled 1643–1715) was at the height of his power, but unfortunately, that was the only height he could claim. You see, the Sun King, one of the most beloved monarchs in history, was—how should I say it?—short. Since the cards were stacked against him in the height department, he decided to use stacks to even things out—he added a few inches to the heels of his boots. The elevator shoes elevated his stature, but he got knocked down a few pegs when he noticed he'd started a fad in his Royal Court—soon everyone was wearing elevator shoes. Not to be overshadowed, Louis added even more height to his heels, and the Royal Court followed suit. Soon people were tottering around in footwear resembling the Frankenstein monster at a disco. Eventually, men's heel size came back to earth, but women stayed perched on high. In the 1800s, American women began emulating the exotic styles of Paris, and soon "French heels" became part of the American fashion scene and were referred to simply as "high heels."

***

Who won the Tony Award for the Best Supporting
or Featured Actor category in 1950? No one.
The judges for the award decided no Broadway performance
was worthy of that award.

Bunker or Just Bunk?

The Battle of Bunker Hill is where the American colonists faced the English in the Revolutionary War and kicked a little redcoat butt, right? Actually, there are two untruths about this statement:

1. The British troops, even though they sustained more casualties, ultimately whipped the Americans, chased them off, and claimed victory in the battle.
2. There was no Battle of Bunker Hill.

Wait, if there was no battle of Bunker Hill, what was all the fighting about? The American troops had orders to protect Bunker Hill, but as is sometimes the case during a war, someone screwed up. The soldiers wound up trying to protect nearby Breed's Hill. So the history books almost got it right: The Battle of Bunker Hill was actually fought on Breed's Hill, and the British won the battle, not the colonists.

It's called a *flea market* because in the olden days most secondhand items had fleas, right? Actually, the term *flea market* comes from Dutch colonial days and their *vallie* (valley) markets. Over the years, *vallie* was shortened to *vlie* (pronounced "flee"), and eventually this got Americanized to *flea*.

Nuclear Arms Wrestling

While performing routine maintenance on a Titan III ICBM silo in September 1980, an Air Force repairman accidentally dropped a wrench socket. The socket bounced off the wall of the Damascus, Arkansas, silo and banged into the missile. Surely a little socket couldn't do any damage to a multimillion-dollar state-of-the-art rocket armed with a nuclear warhead? But the repairman watched in horror as the socket socked the pressurized fuel tank and started a leak. The entire missile complex and surrounding area was evacuated, and eight hours later, a massive explosion rumbled from the silo and blew the 740-ton hatch into the air, followed closely by the nuclear warhead. People watched in terror as the warhead flew 600 feet in the air—but that wasn't the scary part. The scary part was watching the warhead plummeting toward the earth. Amazingly, the warhead didn't explode, but the accident still claimed one life, and eleven other people were injured. This proving the old saying, "One nuclear bomb can ruin your whole day."

❧

Prior to 1953, the slogan of L&M cigarettes was
"Just what the doctor ordered."

Bridge over Troubled Water

In 1981, the Intermarine Company of Ameglia, Italy, celebrated after they were awarded a huge contract from the government of Malaysia to build an enormous minesweeper and three military launchers. It was a coup for the company, which specialized in building smaller vessels. "This contract," they thought, "will make us famous." They were right, but for the wrong reasons. Everything went well for Intermarine, and in fact, they finished the project on time and on budget. During the entire two years it took Intermarine to fulfill their contract, they overlooked one small thing—their shipyard was a mile from the Mediterranean on the Magra River. The river was deep and wide enough to accommodate the ships, but farther downriver was the beautiful but tiny Colombiera Bridge, and not one of the ships could navigate under it. The Intermarine Company pleaded with local authorities, promising they would dismantle the bridge and then rebuild it. The shipyard's dreams of further lucrative contracts sank when the town council said no.

It took architects, draftsmen, masons, woodworkers,
and hundreds of laborers ninety years to build the
Church of Corcuetos in Navarrete, Spain.
The day after it was finally completed in 1625, it collapsed.

Who Are We Having for Dinner?

The U.S. government loves passing referendums honoring people or naming buildings or parts of buildings after influential people—it's safe, and it always makes a great photo opportunity. So when a new staff canteen was built in 1977, it gave the U.S. Department of Agriculture the opportunity to commemorate someone of their choice. They chose to honor a famous nineteenth-century Colorado pioneer, Alferd Packer (not "Alfred" Packer). The grand opening ceremony was spectacular, and there was an excited buzz in the air as dignitaries and the press listened when Agriculture Secretary Robert Bergland proudly announced the opening of the Alferd Packer Memorial Dining Facility. "Alferd Packer," Bergland said, "exemplifies the spirit of fare that this Agriculture Department cafeteria will provide." Several months later, and without any fanfare, the cafeteria was renamed. It was brought to the attention of the USDA that the reason Alferd Packer was famous, or infamous, was because he was accused of and tried for murdering and eating five prospectors in 1874. Bon appétit!

In March 2003, as a protest against France's refusal to support the U.S. position on Iraq, the U.S. House of Representatives officially changed the name French fries to "Freedom fries" (and French toast to "Freedom toast," for that matter—but no word on French kissing) in all three House cafeterias. Along the same lines, during World War II, the German-sounding *sauerkraut* was renamed "liberty cabbage."

Random Acts of Kindness

On May 10, 1975, Washington, D.C., hosted Human Kindness Day IV, organized by a nonprofit arts education group called Compared to What, with the support of the D.C. government and the National Park Service. The event attracted a crowd of 125,000 people and featured Stevie Wonder, Graham Central Station, and other popular bands. At a press conference following the event, police announced that there had been 600 arrests, nearly 500 robberies, 150 smashed windows, 120 occurrences of public brawling, 42 looted concession stands, 33 acts of arson, 17 acts of violence toward police officers, and 14 completely demolished cars. Miss Carol Kirkendall, a spokeswoman for the organizers, said that "although sporadic rock-throwing, public mayhem, and purse-snatchings had been a sadness, a lot of beautiful things were going on out there." I guess if you leave the milk of human kindness out in the sun too long, the sour cream of the crop will rise to the top.

War Is Hell

In 1883, the citizens of Lijar, a small town in southern Spain, were infuriated when reports came back that while visiting Paris, King Alfonso XII had been insulted and attacked. The mayor of Lijar, Don Miguel Garcia Saez, and all 300 citizens of the town demanded retribution and declared war on France on October 14, 1883. Not a single shot was fired and not an injury was sustained during the confrontation. Nonetheless, Mayor Saez became known as "The Terror of the Sierras" for this exploit.

Ninety-three years later, in 1976, King Juan Carlos, Alfonso's great-grandson, made a visit to France during which he was treated with great respect. In 1981, the town council of Lijar ruled that "in view of the excellent attitude of the French," they would suspend hostilities and agree to a cease-fire with France. The current mayor of Lijar, Diego Sanchez, said humbly, "We've forgiven them now," making this the first time in two centuries that France fought a war and didn't lose.

The Emperor's New Chair

In the late 1890s, Emperor Menelik II (1844–1913) of Abyssinia (now Ethiopia) learned that electrocution had become the newest method of capital punishment and wanted to prove to his subjects that Abyssinia could execute with the best of them. The emperor ordered three expensive new electric chairs and was shocked to discover they required electricity to work—Abyssinia did not yet have electrical power. The emperor decided to use one of the electric chairs as his throne. Not to let it seem as if he wasn't grounded, his aides spread the claim that the emperor was immune to the killing ways of the white man.

❧

The will of Madame de la Bresse instructed her
life savings of 125,000 francs be used to buy clothing—
not for the poor, but for naked Parisian snowmen.
In 1876, the courts ruled her bequest valid, thereby
making French snowmen the best dressed in the world.

Foaming at the Mouth

In 1970, the marketing people at Procter & Gamble decided it was time to update the design of boxes of Ivory Snow. After a lengthy audition, they found the perfect model, Marilyn Briggs. Briggs, wrapped in a white terry-cloth robe and gazing lovingly at her baby, exuded the innocence and purity the company wanted to portray. Three years and millions of boxes of Ivory Snow later, the company got into a lather when they discovered Marilyn Briggs was actually Marilyn Chambers, the star of such hard-core pornographic films as *Behind the Green Door* and *Insatiable*. Chambers was one of the superstars of porn from the early 1980s to the early 2000s (originally billing herself as "The Ivory Snow Girl"). I wonder if "getting snowed" had a different meaning back then.

India ink isn't from India, it's actually from China. The French call it Chinese ink.

Survey Says . . .

In the 1880s, as the United States was expanding westward, state borders were rapidly being mapped. After South Dakota's borders were drawn up, two surveyors working toward each other, one from the north and one from the south, began marking out the boundaries. Both men were supposed to follow the same meridian, but the one working his way south missed the surveyor working his way north by about a mile. In order to finish their job, the men decided to join the boundaries with a slight east-west jig—a mistake visible on any map where South Dakota intersects the borders of Montana and Wyoming.

Myth
The chameleon changes color to match its background.

Truth
Chameleons do have the ability to change color instantly, but not to match the color of their surroundings. The color shift is a reaction to fear or extreme changes in temperature or light.

Floundering for a Name

We see tin after tin of sardines in the stores, so it must be pretty easy to catch a sardine, right? Actually, it's impossible to catch a sardine unless you accidentally hook a can lying on the bottom of the sea. Why? Because there's no such fish as a sardine. The name applies to any small fish packaged in sardine cans. (They're usually pilchard or small herring.) The reason sardines are packed, well, like sardines isn't because companies are trying to give you your money's worth—it's because the oil they're packed in costs more than the fish themselves.

In 1986, after thirty-five years on television, the very last scene of the final episode of the daytime soap opera *Search for Tomorrow* had Stu ask Jo what she was "searching" for. To which Jo dramatically replied, "Tomorrow."

Two for One

Has the United States ever had more than one president in power at the same time? Strangely, it has. The presidential race of 1876 between Rutherford B. Hayes and Samuel Tilden was highly contested (a lot like the 2000 race between Al Gore and George W. Bush). Tilden had beaten Hayes by more than 250,000 popular votes, but Hayes won the presidency with one very controversial electoral vote. There was talk of Tilden's group forcibly taking over the White House, and it was a very unnerving time, especially for Hayes. While dining at the White House with President Ulysses S. Grant on the eve of the scheduled inauguration, Grant, Hayes, and Chief Justice Morrison R. Waite quietly excused themselves and went into the Red Room together, where Hayes took the oath of office to forestall any attempted coups. Therefore, technically, both Grant and Hayes were simultaneously president of the United States. The next day, on the east steps of the Capitol, Hayes officially was administered the oath of office. But even if you combine Grant and Hayes, it still would make for one lousy president.

An Eggstraordinary Story

Images of the Virgin Mary on a grilled cheese sandwich, Jesus on a refrigerator door, Mother Teresa on a cinnamon bun—these all seem like laughable bits of weird news. But what if Christ prophesied his return on freshly laid chicken eggs? That's just what happened in a small village near Leeds, England, in 1806, when a hen laid an egg with the words *Christ Is Coming* inscribed in black on its shell. Mary Bateman, the hen's owner, announced that God had arrived in a vision to tell her the hen would lay fourteen prophetic eggs; the fourteenth would usher in the apocalyptic destruction of the world. But the news wasn't all hard boiled—God had also bestowed upon Bateman special slips of paper with the inscription *J.C.* that were basically "Get into Heaven Free" passes available for one shilling apiece. More than 1,000 people purchased the slips of paper and rested comfortably in the knowledge that they were guaranteed salvation while everyone else was going to burn in hell. A doctor who was skeptical of the eggs, or not in on the yolk, examined the eggs and discovered God had used corrosive ink to write on the shells. He told the local authorities, and they burst into the tavern where the chicken was caged and caught Mary Bateman red-handed—shoving the fourteenth inscribed egg into the hen to "lay" later that day. Bateman was hanged, not for egging people into believing her story, but because she later became an abortionist, which was illegal in the nineteenth century.

Birds of a Feather

In November 1977, it wasn't raining cats and dogs, it was actually raining birds. According to eyewitness accounts, approximately 500 dead and dying blackbirds and pigeons dropped on the streets and sidewalks of San Luis Obispo, California, over a period of several hours. As no local spraying had occurred, authorities had no explanation for why the birds had died en masse over their town, giving rise to a different meaning for the phrase "bird droppings."

Arnold Schwarzenegger had competition when auditioning for the lead role in the 1984 film *The Terminator*. O. J. Simpson was seriously considered for the role of cyborg but was eventually dismissed. Why? "People would never have believed a nice guy like O. J. could play the part of a ruthless killer," a studio executive said.

The First Bump in the Road

There's a first time for everything, and Mrs. Bridget Driscoll holds the unfortunate title of being the first person killed by an automobile. On August 17, 1896, at the Crystal Palace in London, Arthur Edsall, an employee of the Anglo-French Motor Car Company, accidentally ran over Mrs. Driscoll and fractured her skull, leading to her death. At the inquest, it was discovered that Mr. Edsall's vision had been obstructed by two other cars, and he could not see Mrs. Driscoll as she crossed the road. The verdict of the court was accidental death. Eyewitnesses stated Mrs. Driscoll panicked at the sight of Mr. Edsall's car and didn't get out of the way, which she could have done easily, as Mr. Edsall was traveling only four miles per hour at the time. So it could basically be called a slow death.

The Mass of Men . . .

The introspective musings of Henry David Thoreau in his book *Walden* are made more romantic by the fact that he voluntarily spent two years isolated from the rest of the world. Well, I hate to burst your literary bubble, but Thoreau's retreat to Walden Pond was more inclusive than reclusive. He built his cabin a scant two miles from his family's home and either strolled into the village, had friends visit him at the pond, or trotted home to raid the family cookie jar nearly every day. Even though his retreat was more like setting up camp in your backyard, you don't have to throw Thoreau away.

Not knowing the name of a particular cape during his voyage up the Bering Strait around 1850, a British officer wrote "? Name" on the map he was creating. When the map was being copied, the mapmaker misread the annotation as "C. Nome," or Cape Nome, and used that name on his map. It was from this geographical mistake that the town of Nome, Alaska, was named.

The Late Winner

Some of the earliest Olympic events made synchronized swimming look about as sissified as, well, synchronized swimming. One such event was called the *pankration*, a mix of boxing, wrestling, and endurance that had virtually no rules. During the pankration event in 564 B.C., Arrachion of Phigalia earned a place in the record books, but not just because he won the bout. Arrachion's opponent, whose name is now forgotten, conceded the event. Arrachion, as he lay on the ground, was declared the winner by default, but he refused to stand and claim victory. Was it because he was exhausted, overcome with the joy of victory, perhaps? No. It was because he was dead. Since the bout had already been decided, Arrachion became the only dead person in history to win an Olympic event. Making the pankration less like a triathlon than a die-athlon.

The 1900 Olympic Games held in Paris included croquet, billiards, archery, cricket, golf, rowing, rugby, soccer, tennis, water polo, tug-of-war, handball, and fishing.

As Good As Gold

As a prospector in Colorado in the 1860s, John Howard was unfamiliar with civil law, but he was well versed in mining laws. So when his wife, Mary E. Howard, sued for divorce, John did not contest it, instead he sent a "quitclaim" deed to the Denver City Court of Chancery.

> *I, John Howard, of Canon City, of the first part, do hereby give, grant, bargain, convey, and quit-claim, all my right, title and interest in the following (un) real estate, to wit:*
>
> *The undivided whole of that ancient estate known as Mary Howard (the title of which I acquired by discovery, occupancy, possession and use), situated at present in the town of Denver, Jefferson Territory, together with all the improvements made and erected by me whereon, with all the rents, profits, easements, enjoyments, long suffering and appurtenances thereto in anywise appertaining, unto _____ of the second part, to have and to hold unto the said _____*
> *so long as he can keep her, without recourse upon the grantor or endorser.*
>
> *In testimony whereof, I have hereunto set my hand, and seal, this, the 24th of January 1861.*
>
> *Signed, JOHN HOWARD*
> *Signed in the presence of A. Rudd, Clerk of District Court.*

You'll notice that John courteously left a blank space in case Mary's future marital prospects panned out.

The monkey wrench was invented by London blacksmith Charles Moncke. When his wrench was brought to the United States, people pronounced its name as a possessive, "Moncke's wrench," which over time became "monkey wrench."

You've Got Mail!

You may never have heard of Alan Ralsky, but you've probably seen his work. Ralsky became a multimillionaire by marketing spam on the Internet. In November 2002, *Detroit Free Press* columnist Mike Wendland wrote a story about Ralsky including the fact that his company sent up to 250 million e-mails a day—the profits from which he used to purchase an 8,000-square-foot, $740,000 home. Ralsky even bragged during the interview that a single weight-loss e-mail paid for an entire wing of his mansion.

A group of anti-spammers who were tired of people like Ralsky making their virtual experience a living hell decided to give Ralsky a taste of his own spam. They posted his home address, e-mail address, and phone number on hundreds of Web sites. Soon Ralsky began receiving literally tons of junk mail, and his inbox was maxed out every morning. What was Ralsky's reaction? The same as ours since people like him began littering the Information Superhighway—he was pissed. "They've signed me up for every advertising campaign and mailing list there is," Ralsky complained. "These people are out of their minds! They're harassing me!" Spam is a revenge best served cold.

❧

The Dead Sea isn't a sea, it's actually a lake.

Up, Up, and Away in My Beautiful Balloon

"What goes up must come down" couldn't be a more fitting phrase for illustrious French inventor Jean-François Pilâtre de Rozier. In 1783, Pilâtre de Rozier, a pioneer in the development of lighter-than-air balloons, became the first person in history to ascend into the heavens in the basket of a hot-air balloon. A few years later, wanting to make history again by being the first person to float across the English Channel, Pilâtre de Rozier created a hybrid balloon consisting of two compartments—one containing hydrogen (a highly explosive lighter-than-air gas), and the other compartment using traditional air heated by an open flame. Theoretically, having an open flame near a highly combustible gas should lead to an explosive disaster, and on June 15, 1785, Pilâtre de Rozier proved that theory correct. About fifteen minutes into his flight, the flame ignited the hydrogen gas, and Pilâtre de Rozier's balloon exploded into flames, plummeting Pilâtre de Rozier's not-lighter-than-air body 3,000 feet to the ground—making him not only the first person to ascend in a balloon but also the first person to die in one.

In a Class by Itself

In 1917, at the height of World War I, the Germans declared unrestricted submarine warfare (sinking merchant ships without warning) in an attempt to cut off trade and supplies to Britain. The British Admiralty decided to produce their answer to the German U-boats—a fleet of 325-foot-long steam-powered submarines called K Class submarines that were soon nicknamed the Kalamity Class. Here's why:

- K1 collided with K4 off the Danish coast on November 18, 1917, and was purposely sunk to avoid capture.
- K2 caught fire on her maiden dive.
- K3 sank for no apparent reason (with the Prince of Wales aboard) and then mysteriously surfaced again.
- K5 was lost due to unknown reasons during a mock battle in the Bay of Biscay on January 20, 1921. The submarine signaled she was diving, and nothing was ever heard from her again.
- K13 sank on January 19, 1917, during sea trials, when an intake failed to close while submerging and her engine room flooded. She was eventually salvaged and recommissioned as K22 in March 1917.
- Two K Class boats were lost in an incident known as the "Battle" of May Island on January 31, 1918. The cruiser HMS *Fearless* collided with the K17 lead submarine, which sank in about eight minutes. In an attempt to get out of the cruiser's way, K4 was struck by K6, nearly cutting her in half, and was then struck by K7 before she finally sank with all her crew.

At the same time, K22 (the recommissioned K13) and K14 collided, although both survived. In a little over an hour and fifteen minutes, two submarines had been sunk, three badly damaged, and 105 crewmembers killed.

- Only one K Class boat ever engaged an enemy vessel, hitting a German U-boat with a torpedo—which failed to explode. In 1918 (after the accidental deaths of some 250 British sailors), the K Class project was abandoned.

People who lived centuries ago weren't as stupid as we may believe they were. Chicken pox isn't called that because people thought the disease was carried by chickens. It comes from the phonetic evolution of the Old English name *gican* ("itching") *pox*.

Come Fly with Me

In the early 1950s, at the height of the Cold War, the Pentagon was an open wallet when it came to defense contractors and newly devised weapons of war. It seemed like all the cool weapons had already been made—so how about a supersonic jet fighter on skis! Enter the Convair F2Y Sea Dart. The jet was devised with a set of retractable skis so it could take off and land without the use of an aircraft carrier. How successful was it? Only five prototypes were made—only three were flown, and only two came back. The first demonstration on April 9, 1953, was called off because the skis caused the plane to shake too violently. For the second demonstration, the plane was fitted with new skis and new engines, and the result was different—it disintegrated in midair in front of navy officials and the press. The Pentagon was embarrassed by the outcome, not because the plane was a failure or because the test pilot had died, but because they had already ordered and paid for twelve F2Y Sea Darts. Convair made millions of dollars, and we got the prequel to the first really fast Jet Ski!

Chalk, the type used on blackboards, is not chalk.
It's calcined gypsum (commonly known as plaster of Paris).

Canvassing History

Close your eyes and imagine (well, read this sentence first, and then close your eyes and see the image of) one of the most famous paintings of American history—*Washington Crossing the Delaware*. It's one of the most recognizable paintings, and one that still stirs the blood of any patriotic American: brave General Washington, standing in the boat, leading his men across the river to surprise the British at the Battle of Trenton on Christmas Eve, 1776. It has all the elements of a true painting of Americana—George Washington, Christmas, and weary soldiers. What it didn't have was its facts straight. A German-American artist named Emanuel Leutze painted the work in 1851, seventy-five years after the battle; he used American tourists as models and the Rhine River for the Delaware. He got the style of the boat wrong, the clothing was incorrect, and even the American flag was wrong (the flag depicted hadn't been created yet). But why let facts get in the way of a little history, right? And hey, it's still a nice painting.

Corned beef has nothing to do with the grain commonly called corn or maize. The *corn* in *corned beef* refers to the "corns" of salt, or rock salt, used in the pickling process of the meat.

Two Kings, Three Queens, and a Big Joker

In 1939, during a trip across Canada, King George VI and his wife, Queen Elizabeth, were greeted by Canadian prime minister MacKenzie King. The mayor of Winnipeg and his wife, Mr. and Mrs. John Queen, also greeted them. So in a bizarre but true variation of Abbott and Costello's famous "Who's on First" routine, here is a partial transcript from the Canadian Broadcasting Corporation announcement of the event:

> There's the King—he's stepping out, followed by Her Majesty Queen Elizabeth, nattily attired in a silver coat. Mr. King is now shaking hands with the King and introducing Mr. Queen to the King and Queen and then Mrs. Queen to the Queen and King. They are now proceeding up the steps to the well-decorated City Hall, the King and Mr. King together, with the Queen being escorted by Mrs. Queen. . . . The King leaves Mr. King and goes to Mrs. Queen, and the Queen and Mr. King follow behind. . . .

When one person is heard constantly complaining, inevitably someone will remark, "Methinks the lady doth protest too much." People do this because they think quoting *Hamlet* makes them sound smart, but it doesn't, because they got the phrase and the meaning wrong. What Gertrude says in *The Tragical History of Hamlet, Prince of Denmark* by William Shakespeare is, "The lady protests too much, methinks," meaning the lady "proclaims" too much, not "complains."

A Sticky Situation

There have been many revolutionary weapons that changed the face of warfare forever: the longbow, the cannon, the Gatling gun, the atomic bomb, and so on. Then there have been weapons that were revolutionary only in their level of stupidity—case in point, Hand Grenade Number 74 (ST). Experts during World War II were confronted with the problem of strategically using hand grenades against tanks. A metal hand grenade hitting a metal tank usually bounced harmlessly off before it exploded. Hand Grenade Number 74 (ST) was the answer, its proud designers bragged, as it was coated with a tacky substance that would stick to the tank. Problem solved. There was, however, one minor problem with using a sticky hand grenade, and that was its tendency to stick to the person throwing it before it stuck to the tank. With only five seconds before detonation, it goes without saying that there were few reorders for Hand Grenade Number 74 (ST). The manufacturer was basically stuck with a huge bomb.

⁂

Horned toads are not toads—they are lizards.

You're Not in Kansas Anymore

They're some of the most famous footwear in history—the ruby red slippers Dorothy wore in *The Wizard of Oz*. But in L. Frank Baum's original novel *The Wonderful Wizard of Oz* (1900), he had her wearing silver slippers. So why did they change it in the movie? Because, when shot in Technicolor, red looked more brilliant than silver.

Myth

IOU stands for "I owe you."

Truth

Who would accept a promissory note that didn't include the lender's name? An IOU from a borrower originally meant "I Owe Unto," followed by the name of the person who loaned the money.

Please Tread Lightly

While we're on the subject of mismatched shoes, in the original story of Cinderella, her infamous glass slippers were actually made of fur. When Charles Perrault finally wrote down the story in 1697 (it had been passed down orally for centuries), he mistook *vair* ("ermine") for *verre* ("glass"). Which makes much more sense, because even though they sound more romantic, glass slippers could cause more damage than just blisters. Perrault realized his mistake, but by that time, the story was so popular, he chose to leave it as it was.

Brass buttons on the sleeves of military uniforms don't actually button up anything, but they do serve a purpose. In 1812, while the French army was sloshing through Russia in the dead of winter, Napoleon grew tired of watching his soldiers wipe their noses with their sleeves. He ordered the brass buttons removed from the uniforms of the dead and sewn onto his soldiers' sleeves in order to curb the habit.

It's a Small World After All

In geography class, we've been taught there are seven continents (Africa, Antarctica, Asia, Australia, Europe, North America, and South America), right? But look at any globe, and you'll see there are really only six (Africa, Antarctica, Australia, Eurasia, North America, and South America). The boundary between Europe and Asia is artificial; ancient Greek mapmakers thought the two regions were separated almost entirely by water from the Aegean to the North Sea. In another case of don't believe what you see but what you've been taught, the incorrect "seven continents" theory is still the norm. This is a case of either tradition beating out the truth or Europeans not wanting to be considered part of Asia.

Church officials, not knowing whether Saint Patrick was born on March 8 or March 9, decided to honor him on March 17, the sum of the two dates.

Nuts to You!

You can buy almonds in their shells, or walnuts in their shells, or Brazil nuts in their shells, so why can't you buy cashews in their shells? For the simple reason that cashews don't have shells. But wait, don't all nuts have shells? That's true, but cashews aren't nuts, they're technically seeds. Peanuts aren't nuts, either; they're actually a species in the legume family.

Jean Baptiste de Chateaubrun (1686–1775) spent
forty years writing, rewriting, and polishing two plays that
virtually constituted his life's work. This was in
the days before Auto-Save, and Chateaubrun became suicidal
when he discovered his housekeeper had carelessly used
the manuscripts as wrapping paper, losing them forever.

The Domino Effect

On June 9, 1978, at New York's Manhattan Center, Mr. Bob Specas was in the final stages of beating a dominoes world record by knocking down 100,000 dominoes in a row. The media was out in droves documenting the historic event. As Specas leaned down to place domino number 97,499 in position, a nearby TV cameraman accidentally dropped his press badge and prematurely set off the dominoes. I'm sure dominoes weren't the only thing that got set off that day—Mr. Specas's temper did, too.

❧

When workmen loaded and stoked the furnaces in Baltimore's newly constructed Howard Hotel in 1912, they quickly learned they had a huge problem stacked against them—the smokestacks. They had forgotten to build chimneys.

What a Stupid Beep, Beep, Beep

The first message sent by Morse code was, "What hath God wrought?" It's a memorable, heartwarming message, but it wasn't the one sent. Samuel Morse's first message was actually, "Everything worked well." It was in a later public demonstration on May 24, 1844, at the Supreme Court Room in the Capitol that Morse sent the memorable message, "What hath God wrought?" It wasn't even Morse's idea to send that particular message—it was Annie Ellsworth, daughter of the commissioner of patents, who suggested it.

> *SOS* in Morse code does not stand for "Save Our Souls,"
> nor does it stand for "Save Our Ship," "Survivors on Ship,"
> "Save Our Sailors," "Stop Other Signals," or
> "Send Out Sailors"—it doesn't stand for anything.
> SOS is the international distress signal:
> three dots/three dashes/three dots all run together.

Descent of the Scent

We've all seen images of people in crowded theaters wearing 3D glasses, but that isn't the only strange movie format that's been created. In the early 1960s, a movie named *Scent of Mystery,* directed by Jack Cardif, incorporated the radical technique called Smellovision. Developed from the Aromarama technique of Charles Weiss, Smellovision accompanied the film with a series of odors that were fed into the theaters' air-conditioning units. Was it popular? Actually, it stank! The aromas from one scene mixed with the odors of the previous scene, leaving theatergoers gagging on a vile stench. The film *Scent of Mystery* was later released as *Holiday in Spain* without Smellovision, but the movie still stank.

Dumb Statements in History

"I guess we'll get through with them in a day."
(General George Custer at Little Big Horn, 1876)

Seldom Is Heard
These Discouraging Words

Everybody sing with me: "Oh, give me a home, where the buffalo roam, and the deer and the antelope play." Americans have sung "Home on the Range" since 1911, so what could possibly be wrong with the song? Well, actually, there are two things:

1. The real home where the buffalo roam is in Africa or Asia (the Cape buffalo of Africa and the water buffalo of Asia). The species we have in the United States is properly called bison.
2. There are no antelope in the United States, either. They're also native to Asia and Africa. What the song calls "antelope" was probably the pronghorn, which is a lot tougher to rhyme. Antelopes grow their horns throughout their lives, whereas pronghorns (*Antilocapridae*) shed their horns annually.

But "Oh give me a home, where the bison roam, and the deer and the pronghorn play" doesn't quite have the same feeling, does it?

❧

Cyndi Lauper's 1984 hit song "Girls Just Want to Have Fun" was written by a man (Robert Hazard).

Really up a Tree

In 1978, British army soldiers were called in to serve as temporary firemen during a strike of local firefighters. An elderly woman called the firehouse on January 14 to ask assistance, as her cat had climbed a tree and was unable to get down. The army arrived quickly and valiantly rescued the woman's cat, placing the purring puss into the woman's grateful hands. So happy was the woman with the army's handling of the situation, she invited the brave men in for tea. They accepted her invitation, and after a pleasant time together, the volunteers bade their host a fond farewell, got back into their fire trucks, and promptly ran over and killed the rescued cat.

To fight off Roman ships in 300 B.C.,
Carthaginians catapulted live snakes at them.

Testing One, Two, . . .

On August 3, 1970, sixty-two-year-old Miriam Hargrave of Yorkshire, England, finally passed her driving test—her fortieth attempt. After so much struggle and perseverance, one would assume she started driving right away. But unfortunately, after spending so much money on driving lessons—$720—she couldn't afford to buy a car. If it took her forty attempts to pass a simple driving test, it's a good thing she never got on the road.

The blindworm, also known as the slowworm or deaf adder, is neither blind nor deaf nor even slow—heck, it isn't even a worm or an adder. The blindworm is actually a legless lizard that can see, hear, and move as quickly as a normal snake.

Not with a Wimper, but with a Bang

On December 6, 1917, the largest man-made explosion of the prenuclear age happened when a ship loaded with munitions exploded in the harbor at Halifax, Nova Scotia, killing more than 1,900 people. The explosion was so massive that one man, William Becker, who was in a rowboat about 300 feet away from the ship when it exploded, was propelled 1,600 yards—the length of sixteen football fields—across the harbor. He was uninjured during his unexpected trip across the harbor and was able to swim to safety—he lived until 1969. Of course, it was difficult to watch football with him: "Sixty-yard touchdown? That's nothing. I once went 1,600 yards for a splashdown!"

Myth
Romans used chariots in battle.

Truth
No. As one must hold on to both reins while
driving a chariot, they were absolutely useless on the battlefield.
Romans used chariots only in sports and as transportation.
Thanks to Hollywood for this myth.

Stupid History

Stop Your Whining

Wine merchant William Sokoin paid $300,000 for a 1787 bottle of Château Margaux once owned by Thomas Jefferson. He planned to sell it to the highest bidder from a group of 300 wine collectors gathered at Manhattan's Four Seasons restaurant in 1989. He hoped to make a profit in excess of $200,000 for the wine, but his dreams were shattered when, moments before the bidding started, he dropped the bottle and broke it.

MTV (Music Television) aired its very first music video,
Video Killed the Radio Star by the Buggles, at midnight,
August 1, 1981. MTV became an overnight phenomenon,
but the Buggles didn't. The group disbanded later in the year.

The Defendants Suck!

In the thirteenth century, the town of Mayenne, France, was infested with a swarm of mosquitoes that plagued the inhabitants to such an extent they filed a lawsuit against them. When the pesky public nuisances flew in the face of authority and refused to answer the summons, the court appointed a lawyer to act on their behalf. The courtroom was abuzz as defense counsel pleaded his case, and spectators waited with bated breath as the judge handed down his verdict. The judge banished the bugs from his jurisdiction, but took pity on them and gave them a patch of land outside the town limits where they could swarm in peace forever. What the townfolks needed wasn't a case against the mosquitoes, but a case of DEET.

❧

Baltimore's prestigious Johns Hopkins University is not named after a Mr. Johns and a Mr. Hopkins—the founder's name was really Johns Hopkins (Johns being a family name).

The Incredible, Regrettable Egg

The citizens of Basel, Switzerland, were stunned when a rooster was accused of laying an egg. In 1473, it was common knowledge that an egg laid by a rooster was prized by sorcerers, and it was known that, according to court records, "Satan employed witches to hatch such eggs, from which proceeded winged serpents most dangerous to mankind." It looked like the rooster's goose was cooked. But even something as foul as a demonic rooster deserves the best defense available, and the court appointed it a lawyer. The lawyer strutted his stuff and contended that "no injury to man or beast had resulted" and that laying an egg is an involuntary act, so, he surmised, his cock should walk.

The judge was impressed with the lawyer's impassioned plea but nonetheless found the rooster guilty of sorcery. Both the rooster and the egg (I'm not sure which one came first) were roasted at the stake—no mention if coleslaw and mashed potatoes were served as sides.

❧

Daniel Decatur Emmett, the man who wrote "Dixie,"
the unofficial anthem of the South, in 1859, was a Northerner.
Emmett was born in Ohio and stayed loyal to the Union
during the Civil War.

Stupid History

A Chili Reception

Christopher Columbus's arrival in the New World is so full of mistakes, it's nearly impossible to categorize them all. One of the most famous is that he thought he had arrived in India, so he called the natives Indians. A lesser-known mistake occurred when his hosts served a spicy food containing hot chilies, which Columbus thought must be related to the *Piper nigrum,* the plant that produces black peppercorns. The spice the Indians actually used wasn't a pepper at all—it was part of the *Solanaceae,* or nightshade, family and was more closely related to potatoes, tomatoes, and eggplants. But thanks to Columbus, chilies have been known as chili "peppers" ever since.

In 1966, instead of airing coverage of the Senate Foreign Relations Committee's hearing on Vietnam, CBS decided to stick with their regularly scheduled programs: reruns of *I Love Lucy, The Real McCoys,* and similar shows.

The Sheep Were Rammed

Nearly 6,000 sheep were drowned when a freighter arriving in a Kuwaiti harbor in 1964 capsized and sank. Authorities knew they needed to remove the carcasses immediately, before the sheep started decomposing and polluting the water. The only way to get the sheep out was to raise the freighter, and that was no small task. Engineers failed to devise a way to raise the tanker in the short amount of time they had before the harbor became polluted. Danish engineer Karl Kroyer was noodling over the problem when he remembered a 1949 Donald Duck comic book, *The Sunken Yacht,* in which Donald and his nephews, Huey, Dewey, and Louie, raised a sunken ship by filling it with table tennis balls. Kroyer thought it was worth a try, and soon the sunken freighter was being filled with twenty-seven million polystyrene balls—and it worked! Another idea was to flood the harbor with Woolite, but everyone thought that was a *baaaaaaad* idea.

The *Mayflower*: Stem to Stern

The Pilgrims were originally heading for Hudson's River, but because of poor navigation and unexpected strong winds, the first land they saw was Cape Cod. The Pilgrims urged the crew of the *Mayflower* to sail further south (yes, there was a crew—the Pilgrims were simply passengers on the *Mayflower*), but "dangerous shoals and roaring breakers" prevented it. By the time the *Mayflower* turned back, the crew was so tired of the Pilgrims' bickering and whining that they dumped them off at the first opportunity, Provincetown, Massachusetts.

During the turbulent times of the Nixon administration, House Minority Leader Gerald Ford was nominated by President Richard M. Nixon to replace Vice President Spiro Agnew, who had resigned. When Nixon himself resigned during the impeachment process for his involvement in Watergate, Ford assumed his duties and became the thirty-eighth president on August 9, 1974, making Gerald Ford the only person to be vice president and president without going through the election process.

Rock and a Hard Place

The Pilgrims docked in Plymouth Harbor after their initial landing, but it's doubtful they landed on Plymouth Rock, since it's not very big. The rock wasn't mentioned by anyone until nearly 100 years after the landing. Thomas Fraunce, a ninety-five-year-old man, claimed his father told him the Pilgrims used the rock to debark from their ship. It's a great story, but Fraunce's father arrived in America three years after the Pilgrims. In an attempt to preserve the rock, it was moved, and in the process, it broke in half. The bottom half, it was decided, could stay where it was. Years later, the rock was put back where it belonged, cemented back to its base, and a monument was built around it. (That's when it was carved with *1620*.) Because of its diminutive size, it is considered one of America's most "disappointing" historical landmarks.

❧

What similarity do human beings and armadillos share?
They are the only two animals that can contract leprosy.

Down the Tube

A nomination in the "whoops" category goes to a worker who, in September 1978, accidentally dropped a 50¢ paint scraper into a torpedo launcher of the U.S. nuclear submarine *Swordfish*, jamming the loading piston. Since the submarine was still at sea, divers worked for a week attempting to free the piston, without success. Ultimately, the *Swordfish* had to be put in dry dock, where repairs ended up costing $171,000. Of course, knowing the government, the 50¢ paint scraper was probably purchased for $171,000, too.

Vincent van Gogh's 1888 painting *The Red Vineyard*
was purchased by Anna Boch of Brussels in May 1890
for 400 francs. It is the only painting Van Gogh sold
during his lifetime.

A Feather in His Cap

"Yankee Doodle" is a strange little ditty that has stayed in the American culture since pre–Revolutionary War times. You know the tune:

> "Yankee Doodle went to town
> A-riding on a pony
> Stuck a feather in his hat
> And called it macaroni."

The rhyme was actually composed in England and was originally an anti-colonist song. *Yankee,* of course, was an American colonist. *Doodle,* according to English dictionaries of the time, meant "a sorry, trifling fellow; a fool or simpleton." *Macaroni* refers not to a pasta dish, but to a foppish and bombastic style of Italian clothing. So basically, the English were saying, "Hey, look at the stupid, country-bumpkin colonist who thinks he's stylish." Strangely enough, "Yankee Doodle" became the colonists' rallying anthem for the Revolutionary War and was used as a marching song. So maybe we were Yankee Doodles after all.

He Said, She Said

In the repertoire of every bad Humphrey Bogart impersonator is the line, "Play it again, Sam." But Bogart never said this. In the 1943 movie *Casablanca*, Ingrid Bergman's character, Ilse, not Humphrey Bogart's, Rick, is the one who implores Sam (Dooley Wilson) to "play it, Sam. Play 'As Time Goes By.'" So no one ever says, "Play it again, Sam," and in fact, Sam never plays "As Time Goes By," he just sings it—Wilson couldn't play the piano, and the accompaniment was dubbed over later.

❧

Patent leather, invented in 1829, has the distinction
of being the only product or process named after
the U.S. Patent Office.

A Revolutionary Item Up for Sale

During the tumultuous and momentous transformation of the Soviet Union in November 1991 from communism to democracy, it seemed like anything could happen—and *Forbes* magazine got the scoop of the century. Apparently, in order to cleanse itself of any memory of communist control and to raise money, the new Soviet government declared that the embalmed remains of Vladimir Ilich Ulyanov—better known as Lenin, the first leader of Soviet Russia and creator of the communist ideology known as Leninism—would be auctioned off to the highest bidder. *USA Today*, the Associated Press, and other news organizations covered the story. ABC's *World News Tonight* with Peter Jennings reported the story and announced that the former communists wanted to capitalize on the capitalists, stating, "They won't consider anything less than $15 million [for Lenin's body]." Talk about that hard-to-find gift for the person who has everything. The following evening, Jennings broke in with an important update on the special Red sale—it was a hoax. "We said it was an extraordinary story," Jennings said apologetically. "More to the point, it wasn't true. We were gullible, and we assure you that the next report . . . is no joke." In case you were wondering, Lenin's preserved body is still on display at the Lenin Mausoleum in Moscow, and if there's any tag on him, it's a toe tag, not a sales tag.

New World, Old Lie

Christopher Columbus gets a lot of credit for things he never did—like discovering America. And I'm not making the politically correct argument that he couldn't "discover" a continent when there were people already living there. What I'm saying is that Columbus didn't "discover" America because he never actually set foot on the American mainland. When Columbus sailed the ocean blue in 1492, he landed on Watlings Island in the Bahamas. In his three subsequent excursions across the Atlantic, his landings were all in South America and the Caribbean. The explorer who actually discovered the continental United States was Juan Ponce de León, who set foot in Florida in 1513. Columbus, who was convinced he had reached Asia, never claimed to have discovered the New World. Although America wasn't named for Christopher Columbus, I'm glad it wasn't named for Ponce de León, either—I wouldn't want to live in Leónville.

We've all heard of London's famous
Big Ben—but what is it? Is it the clock?
Is it the tower? Nope, it's neither. Big Ben
is the name for the thirteen-and-a-half-ton
bell inside the clock tower. It was cast in
1858 and named in honor of Sir Benjamin
Hall, who served as commissioner of works
when the bell was installed.

Bending the Amendment

In any debate over prayer in school, Nativity scenes or Christmas trees on state property, or statues of the Ten Commandments in courthouses, the "wall of separation between church and state as outlined in the Constitution" is bound to be brought up. Which is an interesting argument because there is no "wall of separation between church and state" mentioned anywhere in the Constitution or the Bill of Rights. The First Amendment states only that "Congress shall make no law respecting an establishment of religion, or prohibiting the free exercise thereof." The Founding Fathers included this amendment because they didn't want the United States to establish a national church (like the Church of England)—one of the reasons the Founding Fathers took the time to write everything down—but no one, not even the courts, takes the time to read it.

Electric eels are not eels. They are a freshwater fish native to South America and are related to the carp.

It Isn't Made of Cheese, Either

The "dark side of the moon" sounds like a daunting, frightening, mysterious, and terrifying place—and it would be, if it existed. Although it's true that the same side of the moon always faces the earth, that doesn't mean the other side is always dark. Every acre of the moon is illuminated at one time or another. However, if the phrase "dark side of the moon" didn't exist, we might not have one of the best rock albums in history.

Head cheese is not a type of cheese—it's not even a dairy product. Head cheese is boiled and coarsely chopped meat from the head of a calf or pig (sometimes a sheep or cow) and may also include meat from the heart or feet. The boiled meat is then mixed with gelatin, shaped in a mold to resemble cheese, and served cold.

W. C. Fields Forever

"Anybody who hates children and dogs can't be all bad" is the perfect quote to embody the comedian W. C. Fields (William Claude Dukenfield), and it's one of his most famous sayings, but like most things in this book, it's a myth. The actual quote is "Anybody who hates dogs and babies can't be all bad." This misquote wouldn't be enough to include by itself if not for the fact that W. C. Fields never said either line in the first place. The original quote came from Leo Rosten, the humor writer, who said it when introducing Fields at a dinner. Unfortunately for Mr. Rosten, W. C. Fields is still given credit for this great line.

❧

Koala bears are not bears. They are marsupials like kangaroos, opossums, Tasmanian devils, and wallabies, all having a pouch where their newly born baby ("joey") develops.

Exit, Stage Left!

 W. C. Fields has been falsely credited with several events and quotes—even after his death. Included in most nonfiction stories of Fields is the epitaph on the vault housing his ashes, "On the whole, I'd rather be in Philadelphia." It would be a great ending to the comedian's career, but it's not true. In fact, Fields never even said this line—it actually appeared as a joke in the magazine *Vanity Fair* in the 1920s and was assigned to Fields after his death. What is on his grave marker in Forest Lawn Memorial Park Cemetery? His name and his birth and death years.

Welsh rabbit has nothing to do with rabbits. In the seventeenth and eighteenth centuries, the adjective *Welsh* meant something of inferior quality. So if someone couldn't snare a rabbit for dinner, he or she might have had to settle for Welsh rabbit— melted cheese on toast.

Structured Chaos

In 1976, the American Institute of Architects awarded the Kemper Arena in Kansas City their prize as "one of the finest buildings in the nation." So it was no surprise when on June 3, 1979, they decided to hold their annual conference near the arena. On the first day of the conference, architects toured this awe-inspiring structure, noting, in particular, the wide-spanning roof trusses, which the *Architectural Record* described as having "an almost awesome muscularity."

On the second day, a major storm hit Kansas City, with winds in excess of seventy miles per hour. Soon the architects' awe turned into "ahhh!" when the roof of "one of the finest buildings in the nation" collapsed. Apparently, the bolts used in the roof hangings weren't strong enough to support the wind, the rain, and the roof at the same time. So because of a bad bolt, the whole arena got screwed.

Holy Santa Maria!

As I've mentioned before, Christopher Columbus's journeys to the New World were fraught with mistakes, miscalculations, misinterpretations, and miscellaneous mischief. Here are but a few examples:

- The main reason Columbus was so confident he could reach Asia was that he had underestimated the earth's circumference by 7,600 miles.
- Not realizing he had discovered a new continent, he never bothered naming it—so a less-significant explorer, Amerigo Vespucci, decided to name it for him—America.
- Columbus searched in vain for gold and treasure but never found any. He did make one interesting trade with the Indians—his crew infected them with smallpox and, in exchange, the Indians presented the Europeans with syphilis.

A Close Shave

Hans Steininger was a famous politician in Brünn, Austria, not necessarily for any legislation, but because his beard was longer than he was tall—it was reportedly the longest beard in the world. But his beard's growing days were cut short in September 1567, when while climbing the steps leading to the council chamber, he tripped over his beard, fell down the stairs, and died. It's like the old saying, "Hair today, gone tomorrow."

Whalebone, used in the nineteenth century for buggy whips, parasol ribs, and corset stays, is not bone at all. It is baleen, a stiff but somewhat elastic substance made of keratin (the same stuff that's in our fingernails, teeth, and hair) found in the upper jaws of baleen whales.

Stupid History

Cue the Crying Indian!

Earth Day, April 22, 1990, was celebrated by hundreds of thousands of people gathered in New York's Central Park to express their support for environmental programs. When the event was over, more than memories were left behind—fifty park sanitation workers picked up an estimated 1,543 tons of litter the concerned demonstrators had left behind.

❧

The English horn is neither English nor a horn.
Its origins are in the Near East, and it
was improved and redeveloped in Vienna.
It is a woodwind in the oboe family.

Like a Rolling Stone

A stone with mysterious etchings was uncovered by archae-
ologists among prehistoric Native American relics in the Grave
Creek Mound in West Virginia in 1838. Over the next century, the
stone continued to stump scientists and more than sixty linguists, who
were unable to decipher the strange carving. In 1930, a young man
photographing the famous mystery from a variety of angles accidentally
discovered the solution. Like the popular optical illusion puzzles in
which greatly elongated letters can be read only when they're viewed
at an extreme angle, the photograph solved the nearly 100-year-old
mystery. The carving on the stone read:

BILL STUMP'S STONE
October 14, 1838

Making one wonder if the legend meant it was a stone by Bill
Stump or if Bill knew his stone would stump people.

Roses on Your Piano

Pokémon, Beanie Babies, Cabbage Patch Kids, and tulips are all examples of collectible "crazes." Yes, tulips. Tulips were introduced into Holland in the late 1500s and were much sought after by the upper class. In 1634, traders began speculating on tulip bulbs, and soon the price of certain prized tulips skyrocketed—the age of tulipmania had struck! The rare Semper Augustus sold for as much as 5,500 florins per bulb, the equivalent of eight pounds of gold. But eventually, the tulip bubble burst, and in February 1637, the price of bulbs hit the dirt. Thousands of people went bankrupt, and investors refused to honor the futures contracts they had signed. When these cases went to court, they were ruled to be gambling debts, not enforceable contracts. I guess in this case it wasn't money but tulip bulbs that were the root of all evil.

Auguste Rodin's famous bronze sculpture referred to as *The Thinker* wasn't what the artist was thinking about. Rodin originally named his sculpture *The Poet,* as it depicts Dante Alighieri, the author of *The Divine Comedy*, sitting in front of the gates of hell contemplating his great poem. An unknown art critic who was unfamiliar with Dante's work referred to the statue as *The Thinker,* and the name caught on.

Sitting in Judgment of Yourself

The Pacific Gas & Electric Company was on trial in Nevada City, California, in 2000 charged with "failing to trim vegetation around power lines." The trial was delayed for more than thirty minutes when the power to the town was accidentally cut off—a tree branch had fallen and knocked down a power line. It's events like these that strengthen my belief in God—and that he's got a sense of humor.

"At the end of every rainbow, you'll find a
pot of gold." It's something we all think about
at one time or another when we see a rainbow,
but that's not how the original saying went. In the
thirteenth century, a common saying was,
"One would be as likely to find a pot of gold as
to find the end of a rainbow," which makes sense.
The Irish borrowed from this saying and crafted it
into their leprechaun mythology.

Roll It

It's assumed that sunny California became the home to early filmmakers because it's, well, sunny. Motion picture cameras of the day required a lot of light, and it was less expensive to shoot outdoors than in a studio. But these pioneers of the picture show weren't just looking for a place in the sun, they were also looking for a place to hide. You see, Thomas Edison owned the patent on the film camera, and these filmmakers were infringing on Edison's patent. Southern California became the perfect location because it was as far away from Edison's lawyers as one could get and still stay in the United States. If the lawyers "went West," it was a simple matter for these filmmakers to escape to Mexico.

A Close Call

In July 1956, a B-47 Stratojet subsonic bomber crashed into a storage igloo twenty miles south of Cambridge, England. The plane burst into flames on impact but surprisingly didn't ignite the contents of the igloo. A lucky day for the citizens of Cambridge, because the igloo contained three Mark Six nuclear bombs.

Until 1937, consumption and sale of cannabis
(as hemp for clothing and rope and in cigarette form)
was made illegal without the purchase of
a federal tax stamp. Congress didn't think it had the
authority to outlaw a plant, so they imposed a hefty
tax instead. This reduced the amount of trade,
but apparently not enough. To legally make
marijuana illegal, Congress simply stopped issuing
the tax stamp, and without a tax stamp, it was illegal
to buy or sell cannabis.

Don't Want No Fancy Funeral, Just One Like Old King Tut

On November 4, 1922, archaeologist Howard Carter made one of the greatest archaeological finds in history when he discovered the virtually untouched tomb of Tutankhamen, the Egyptian boy king, who lived around 1350 B.C. The tomb of King Tut, in the Valley of the Kings, was so filled with artifacts, it took nearly ten years to catalog them all. But one, the most stupefying and mind-boggling artifact of them all, was reported on by Charles Langdon Clarke of the *Toronto Mail and Empire*—it was King Tut's "golden typewriter." Yes, a solid-gold typewriter was found among the thousands of other priceless items in the tomb. A rival newspaper sent a reporter to interview noted Egyptologist Dr. C. T. Currelly, curator of the Royal Ontario Museum, to discuss the earth-shattering discovery. Once Clarke realized someone was going to follow up on his story, he decided to release his source: himself. Clarke confessed that the golden typewriter was a hoax. What's odd is that no one questioned how the golden typewriter could print hieroglyphics and how a machine could be built large enough to hold all the symbols. But what's stranger than that is, of all the truly amazing and real artifacts discovered in the tomb, why would someone want to make up a fake one?

A Twist of Lemming

Contrary to popular myth, lemmings do not commit mass suicide. The origin of this lemming tale is traced to the 1958 Walt Disney film, *White Wilderness.* One scene shows a dozen lemmings scurrying toward the edge of a cliff, where they "dutifully toss themselves over a cliff into certain death in icy Arctic waters." Believe it or not, the filmmakers staged the suicide scene, but when the lemmings refused to go voluntarily over the cliff, they were tossed over by the film crew. "Gradually strength wanes . . . determination ebbs away . . . and the Arctic Sea is dotted with tiny bobbing bodies," concludes the narrator.

You would think the Disney Company, which made its fortune off a mouse, would be kinder to its relatives.

Even though footballs are called "pigskins," they are not made from pigskins but from cowhide.

Sax and Violins

Catgut, which for centuries has been used to string musical instruments, is made from cats, right? Not even close. *Catgut* is a term for a chemically treated animal intestine made into a tough string or cord. But the animal in question isn't a cat and never has been; it's a sheep. So why isn't it called sheepgut? Good question. Here's my guess: Imagine the sound of a young child practicing a violin, and then imagine the sound of a cat with its tail caught in a door. The word *catgut* makes a lot more sense now, doesn't it?

The pineapple is almost exclusively identified with Hawaii, but the fruit is not native to the islands. Our old friend Christopher Columbus picked up a few in the Caribbean in 1493, and because they looked like great big pinecones, he called them the "Pine of the Indies." The English compared the sweet taste to an apple, and soon the fruit was called a pineapple. They became all the rage in England and were introduced to Hawaii when Captain James Cook took some with him on an expedition circa 1770.

It's a Dog's Life

When calculating the age of old Fido, most people use the equation one human year equals seven dog years. But if you think about that logic for only a moment (four hours in dog moments), you'll see it doesn't hold true. Using this theory, Bluey, an Australian cattle dog who lived to be twenty-nine years old, would have been 203 years old in human years. So how do you compare a dog's age in human years? Since puppies become dogs much quicker than babies become adults, the equation could be figured more along these lines: fifteen years for the first year of the dog's life, ten years for the second, seven for the third, and three for each following year. Making a three-year-old dog thirty-two, a fourteen-year-old dog sixty-five, and our twenty-nine-year-old dog an amazing but more realistic 110 years old. Of course, it's much harder for a dog to figure out the age of a human in dog years.

Covering Up the Past

Can you imagine someone taking a beautiful piece of white marble Greek statuary and painting it in flesh tones, making its hair black or brown, coloring the clothing, or if the statue was naked, painting in pubic hair? That would be considered vulgar and uncouth, but that's what the Greeks did. Statues in ancient times weren't cold, bland, white likenesses of gods, royalty, and nobles—they were colorfully painted and left no detail to the imagination. Even busts were painted—and sculptures of people's heads were, too!

Bald eagles aren't bald, so how did they get their name? In Middle English, *balded* meant "white," and over the years, the word was shortened to *bald*. That's why the American eagle, with its white-feathered head, is called the bald eagle. *Pibald* ("part white") is used to refer to dogs with white spots.

Alone Again, Naturally

Let's get this straight: Charles Lindbergh was not the first to fly nonstop across the Atlantic. The first nonstop flight was made on June 14, 1919, by John Alcock and Arthur Whitten Brown, and if you count two earlier dirigible crossings transporting a total of sixty-four people, Lindbergh was actually the sixty-seventh person to cross the Atlantic. The key word missing from these previous accomplishments is *solo*. On May 21, 1927, Charles Lindbergh was the first person to fly nonstop across the Atlantic, from the United States to Europe, by himself. I suppose if people could remember his nickname, "The Lone Eagle," they wouldn't get things confused.

❦

A "moment" technically lasts ninety seconds.

Ship Faced

It was one of the most historic battles of the Civil War—the four-hour Battle of Hampton Roads on March 9, 1862, between the two ironclads the *Monitor* and the *Merrimac*. What makes this battle easily memorable is that both ships' names started with the letter *M*. The problem is, the *Monitor* didn't fight the *Merrimac*, it fought the *Virginia*. The *Merrimac* was a typical U.S. Navy wooden frigate built in 1856 that was set on fire so as not to be confiscated by Confederate forces. The Rebels salvaged the ship, cut off its upper hull, and outfitted it with sloping metal sides, rechristening it the CSS *Virginia,* and it was under that name that it battled the *Monitor.* In 1995, the U.S. Postal Service commemorated the battle with a 32¢ "Monitor * Virginia" stamp and was inundated with calls and letters telling them they had screwed up.

❧

A steel-jacketed bullet is actually made of brass.

Petite Defeat

Three things are usually remembered about Napoleon Bonaparte: his big, funny hat; having his hand inside his vest; and the fact that he was short. Even now, hyperaggressive, height-impaired men are said to have a Napoleon complex. This would come as a surprise to the emperor of the French, because he actually stood five feet six and a half. The confusion about Napoleon's size arose because after his autopsy, it was reported that he measured five feet two. The problem is, he was measured based on the old French system of *pied de roi* ("royal foot"), which was shorter than the modern foot. The height requirement for the French army at the time was four feet eleven, so a lot of Napoleon's soldiers looked up to the great conqueror not because of his powerful position, but because he was taller than they were. Napoleon wasn't short, and he certainly wasn't shortsighted when he said, "History is a set of lies agreed upon."

❧

The infamous battle of Waterloo wasn't fought in Waterloo. Napoleon's defeat occurred outside the village of Pancenoit, which was over four miles away.

Going Postal

If "neither rain nor snow nor heat nor gloom of night stays these couriers from the swift completion of their appointed rounds" is the official motto of the U.S. Postal Service, why is the mail service cancelled during a blizzard? The simple answer is, the Postal Service doesn't have a motto. This famous quote, by Greek historian Herodotus (circa 500 B.C.), was actually written about the mounted postal couriers of ancient Persia. Since there's not a lot of great quotes about mail carriers, I suppose the designers of the New York City post office settled for this one and engraved it along the top of the building.

King Charles VIII of France, after ascending to the throne in 1483, became paranoid with the thought of someone trying to poison him. As a result, he began eating less and less and suspecting people more and more.
But all that ended in 1498, when the king died not of poisoning, but of malnutrition.

The Big Bus Fuss

Why aren't there electric streetcars anymore? The answer: General Motors. In the 1930s, GM was looking for a way to expand its bus manufacturing business, but buses weren't needed in most cities, because they already had electric streetcar or trolley lines. So GM, along with Standard Oil, Firestone Tires, and several other corporations, formed a company to buy municipal streetcar systems and dismantle them. After a few trial cities, their plan seemed to be working, so they moved on to New York and Los Angeles. In April 1949, a Chicago federal jury convicted GM, Standard Oil, and Firestone of criminally conspiring to replace electric transportation with buses and monopolizing the sale of buses—they were fined $5,000. So it's not only the bus fumes that stink!

Speakin' Lincoln

When one thinks about President Abraham Lincoln, the image of a tall, bearded, deep-voiced man comes to mind. Well, he was tall and bearded, but he didn't have a deep voice. In fact, Lincoln's voice was actually high-pitched, shrill, and piercing. Not a very good attribute for today's politicians, but during the days of open-air speeches and debates, Lincoln's voice could be heard clearly hundreds of yards away, while his opponent's faded off. He was an excellent speechwriter as well, and rarely spoke out of his hat.

Myth

Karate is a traditional Japanese martial art.

Truth

No. Karate originated in India and spread to China before reaching Japan. The word *karate* is pronounced the same way in both Japanese and Chinese. In Japanese, *karate* means "empty hand"; in Chinese, it means "Tang dynasty hand."

A Penny for Your Thoughts

"You can fool all of the people some of the time and some of the people all of the time, but you can't fool all of the people all of the time" is a quote made famous by President Abraham Lincoln, right? Sorry. This remark is not found in any of the writings of Abraham Lincoln, nor can it be found in any newspapers from Lincoln's time. In fact, the saying did not surface until more than fifty years after Lincoln was supposed to have said it. Most historians now attribute the remark to circus impresario P. T. Barnum. But nearly 150 years later, it seems this old saying isn't even true—all of the people were fooled for all of this time.

You Must Have the Wrong Address

Although the Gettysburg Address is considered the most eloquent oration in U.S. history, the *Chicago Times* hated it. On November 20, 1863, the day after Lincoln delivered his famous speech, the *Times* wrote:

> The cheek of every American must tingle with shame as he reads the silly, flat and dish-watery utterances of the man who has been pointed out to intelligent foreigners as the President of the United States.

᭜

Levi Strauss didn't call his creation blue jeans or even jeans. He called them "waist overalls."

Horsing Around with History

The Pony Express is a highly romanticized portion of an already overly romanticized period in American history. But the real story of the Pony Express, which lasted only eighteen months, comes up lame. It was too expensive to use and too expensive to run. And being a rider for the Pony Express wasn't a glamorous job, either. Just look at the newspaper want ads from that time:

> *Wanted: Young, skinny fellows, not over eighteen. Must be expert riders willing to risk death daily. Orphans preferred. Wages $25 per week. Apply Central Overland Express.*

What finally pulled in the reins on the Pony Express was Samuel Morse's transcontinental telegraph line, finished in 1861. The Pony Express was put out to pasture almost overnight, with over $500,000 in debt.

❧

Not a single pony was used in the Pony Express. Ponies didn't have the strength or endurance to make the 2,000-mile journey—but Horse Express just didn't sound right.

Not in High Cotton

Eli Whitney is credited with inventing the cotton gin in 1794 and single-handedly saving the South's cotton industry. Before his invention, it took an entire day for one person to separate a single pound of cotton from the seeds. After only a few days of experimenting, Whitney came up with a simple, efficient machine that made the work of separating cotton easy. In 1792, the United States exported approximately 140,000 pounds of cotton; by 1800, because of Eli Whitney's cotton gin, that number went up to 18 million pounds. So this simple machine must have made Mr. Whitney a lot of cotton-picking money, right? No. The machine was so simple that any farmhand could easily copy it . . . and they did. Companies began producing their variations of the cotton gin, but even though Whitney took them to court over patent infringement, the courts consistently ruled against him. After thirteen years of fighting court battles over his design that saved Southern agriculture, Whitney finally got a favorable ruling in 1807—but by then, the patent had nearly expired. And soon after that, Mr. Whitney expired, too.

Buckle Up

Were the Puritans pure of spirit and body? Hardly. There are hundreds of court records documenting cases of sodomy, rape, adultery, fornication, and other not-so-pure deeds. Like this one: On September 8, 1642, a sixteen-year-old from Plymouth, Massachusetts, was hanged because of his love for animals. "Thomas Granger was detected of buggery with a mare, a cowe, two goats, five sheep, two calves and a turkey," as Governor William Bradford wrote in *Of Plimouth Plantation, 1620–1647*. "And whereas some of the sheep could not be so well known by his description of them, others with them were brought before him and he declared which they were and which they were not." To make matters worse for young Granger, he had to watch the objects of his affection die first. "A very sade spectacle it was; for first the mare, and then the cowe, and the rest of the lesser cattle, were kild before his face, according to the law, Leviticus 20:15, and then he him selfe was executed." All this because the guy was caught horsing around.

Keeping an Eye Out

In 1801, Captain Horatio Nelson of the British navy was engaged in attacking French troops in Copenhagen, Denmark. The tide of the battle turned in favor of the French, and Nelson was ordered by the command ship to retreat. But Nelson wanted to continue fighting and ignored the command. A subordinate urged the captain to heed the commander's order, and Nelson picked up a telescope to verify the signal for himself. But Nelson, who was blind in one eye, purposely held the telescope to his sightless eye and said truthfully that he "couldn't see" any signal of retreat. Nelson continued his attack and won. This event left us with a phrase that means "to ignore something" and is still used today: to turn a blind eye.

One thing you might notice while visiting any of the Disney theme parks is the total lack of facial hair. Disney has banned any of its employees from wearing a beard, mustache, soul-patch, imperial, or any other type of facial hair. The only person ever allowed to have face-fuzz was Walt Disney himself. You can call this archaic rule crazy—or just call it goofy.

The Case of Coke

Coca-Cola is not only an American institution, it's one of the most successful businesses in American history. John Pemberton, a pharmacist in Atlanta, concocted the drink in 1886, for use as a nonalcoholic "nerve medicine." And yes, the first recipe included coca leaves—along with kola nuts and other herbs. Pemberton would then mix the thick syrup with tap water and sell it in his drugstore. The story is that a customer, complaining of an upset stomach, asked Pemberton to mix the syrup with carbonated water, and it was at that moment that the pharmacist realized he had "the real thing." So Pemberton began producing Coke and retired a billionaire—well, if he did, he wouldn't be in this book. Shortly after he created the drink, Pemberton became very sick, and in desperate need of money, he sold the rights to Coke to a group of druggists for about $350. He died of cancer in 1888. Pemberton went from soft drinks to hard times.

Its What's for Supper

We've all heard the expression "It's raining cats and dogs," but how about the phrase "It's raining meat!" You would be familiar with this phrase if you were in southern Bath County, Kentucky, on Friday, March 3, 1876. While in her yard making soap, Mrs. Allen Crouch was sprinkled with dime-size pieces of fresh meat, and there wasn't a meat cloud in the sky. Two gentlemen who tasted the meat agreed it was either mutton or venison. During examination, scientists concluded the first sample was lung tissue from a horse or a human baby. (I didn't know they were so similar.) Further samples were identified as cartilage and striated muscle fibers. No definitive explanation for the meat shower was given, but one theory was that a flock of buzzards had thrown up while flying over Mrs. Crouch's yard. What is so weird about this story is the two men who volunteered to taste the meat.

Oscar Hammerstein II is the only person in history named Oscar to win an Oscar. In fact, he won two (in 1941 for his lyrics to "The Last Time I Saw Paris," from *Lady Be Good,* and in 1945 for his lyrics to "It Might as Well Be Spring," from the film *State Fair*).

Piercing the President

In 1853, President Franklin Pierce, widely known for his losing battle with the bottle, was arrested in Washington, D.C., after he accidentally ran down an elderly lady, Mrs. Nathan Lewis, with his horse. Mrs. Lewis wasn't injured, but Constable Stanley Edelin placed the president in custody. No matter what kind of executive privileges the president has, the U.S. Constitution doesn't give the president immunity from arrest. Mrs. Lewis was in stable condition, Pierce's horse was placed in a stable, and the president's term of office was unstable at best.

Eugene Debs is the only person in history to run a presidential race while serving time in prison. He ran on the Socialist Party ticket in 1920, gaining 920,000 votes but losing to Warren G. Harding. Debs was serving a ten-year sentence for publicly criticizing the government's questionable use of the Espionage Act in prosecuting people.

Get a Tan by Standing in the English Rain

In many Mediterranean countries, solar-powered city parking meters are used, saving a fortune in maintenance costs. So city officials in Nottingham, England, decided to get in on this action and spent more than £1 million (about $1.5 million) installing solar-powered parking meters on their city streets. There was one glaring problem Nottingham officials overlooked—or should I say a problem that wasn't glaring—the sun. Mediterranean countries get a lot of sun, and even in the summer, England doesn't. As of August 2001, more than 245 of the parking meters were out of commission, allowing hundreds of motorists to park for free.

Because she is a member of the royal family and not a commoner, the queen of England is not allowed to enter the House of Commons.

Cast the First Stone

Dr. Johannes Beringer, dean of the University of Würzburg's medical school, astounded the scientific community in 1725 by announcing the discovery of hundreds of tiny fossils along with a number of clay tablets, including one, he claimed, "signed by Jehovah." Thrilled with his discovery, Dr. Beringer published a book the following year based on the hypothesis that both the tablets and the fossils were carved by the hand of God. The book sent shock waves through the academic world, but soon rumors bubbled to the surface. J. Ignatz Roderick, a geography professor, and Georg von Eckhardt, the university's librarian, admitted that they had carved the stones themselves as a cruel joke—they even carved Beringer's name on one of the stones. Instead of admitting he had fallen victim to a hoax, Beringer attempted to buy up all copies of his book. When word got out of what he was doing, the book suddenly became a collector's item, carving out a little place in stupid history for Dr. Johannes Beringer.

Scooping It Up

All newspapers and news programs try to get the scoop on big stories, and occasionally, in their haste, they overlook a few facts—or blow the story completely. On November 8, 1918, the United Press Association reported that Germany had signed a peace agreement, thereby bringing World War I to an end. Newspapers all across the country began reprinting the organization's story, and celebrations broke out. But the story was wrong. It all started when someone, now believed to be a German secret agent, called the French and American intelligence offices to report that Germany had signed an armistice. The story was passed to Roy Howard, United Press president in Europe, who wired the story to the United States. I'm sure a lot of newspapers were sold that day, but the war didn't officially end until June 28, 1919, with the signing of the Treaty of Versaille.

Get Out of Jail Free

Governor of Georgia Eugene Talmadge is remembered as a segregationist and for his book-banning agenda in state colleges. He was also a man who loved to wield power. When Talmadge was touring the Georgia State Penitentiary in 1936, he asked prisoners, as he passed their cells, one question, "Are you guilty?" The answer to the question always came back an emphatic no. But when he approached the cell door of Leland Harvey and Aubrey Smith, who were serving 150-year terms for armed robbery, he was shocked when both men answered, "Yes!" "It seems you only have two thieves in your penitentiary," Talmadge said to the warden. "I will pardon these two men." Harvey and Smith did indeed receive pardons from the governor, who later explained, "Truthful men should never be confined with a bunch of liars." Sounds like something Congress should think about, too.

Vote, and Vote Often

Charles D. B. King, the incumbent president of Liberia, beat the challenger, Thomas J. Faulkner, by a whopping 600,000 votes in the country's presidential election in 1927. Obviously, the voters had spoken—actually, more than just the voters had spoken, because there were only 15,000 registered voters at the time. King was crowned president anyway and earned the dubious achievement of being listed in the *Guinness Book of Records* for the most fraudulent election ever reported in history. This is a prime example of politicians "getting out the vote."

❧

Al Capone ran one of the most ruthless and far-reaching gangs of the prohibition era in the twentieth century—but what did his brother Vincent Capone do? Vincent, Al's older brother, was a police officer in Nebraska.

Bailing Out on War

Wars are started for a variety of reasons: to take over land, to take resources, to avenge a great wrong, to free a repressed people, or to steal a wooden bucket. The War of the Oaken Bucket (1325–1337) was fought between the independent Italian city-states of Modena and Bologna and started when Modena soldiers invaded Bologna to steal a bucket. The raid was successful, but during the ensuing invasion, hundreds of Bologna citizens were killed (or kicked the bucket). Bologna declared war to restore national honor and to avenge the death of the martyred citizens . . . oh, and to get the bucket back. The war raged on for twelve years, but Bologna never did get a handle on the bucket. To this day, it's still in Modena, stored in the bell tower of the twelfth-century cathedral Duomo di Modena.

In Scottish novelist and playwright J. M. Barrie's first book featuring Peter Pan, the 1902 *The Little White Bird*, and the subsequent play from 1904, *Peter Pan, or the Boy Who Wouldn't Grow Up*, Peter Pan flies with the Darling children to "Neverland," not "Never-Never Land." The latter became the popular reference because of the animated Disney film and Mary Martin's popular musical adaptation in the early 1950s.

A Fork in the Family Tree

A man from Lancashire, England, Ian Lewis, spent three decades tracing his family's roots back to the seventeenth century. Lewis traveled extensively in England, interviewing some 2,000 relatives, to map out his genealogy, and he learned something he didn't know: He was adopted. It turned out his real name wasn't Lewis at all, but David Thornton; he had been adopted when he was one month old. Lewis/ Thornton said he would start tracing his new identity immediately after he rooted out why his parents never told him he was adopted.

George M. Cohan is one of the most-beloved composers in American history—giving us such classics as "The Yankee Doodle Boy," which contains the lyrics, "A real live nephew of my Uncle Sam's, / Born on the Fourth of July." Cohan not only wrote these words but claimed July 4 as his birthday, too. But according to his baptismal certificate, apparently Cohan was yanking our doodle—he was born on the third of July, not the fourth, in 1878.

The Winner of the "What Was He Thinking?" Award

Francisco Solano Lopez, president of Paraguay (1862–1870), after a trip to Paris, became obsessed with Napoleon (some say he even believed he was Napoleon). In 1864, to prove he had Napoleon's leadership abilities, he simultaneously declared war on his country's three neighbors: Argentina, Brazil, and Uruguay. The war was also known by three different names: the Napoleonic Wars, the War of the Triple Alliance, and the Paraguayan War. The outcome of the war? Paraguay was nearly annihilated. It is estimated that 90 percent of its population died during the war (as a result of battle, bad food, and disease). There is still debate over whether Lopez was a champion of smaller nations against more powerful neighbors or . . . well, a nut.

Life Imitates Art Imitates Life

The China Syndrome, starring Jane Fonda, Jack Lemmon, and Michael Douglas, was a 1979 film about a near-meltdown at a nuclear power plant. The term *China syndrome* sarcastically refers to highly radioactive fission products overheating and melting through the reactor's container (supposedly melting "all the way to China"). The controversial film sparked fierce debate between anti-nuclear and pro-nuclear groups. One pro-nuke executive for Southern California Edison was quoted as saying, "[The movie] has no scientific credibility, and is in fact ridiculous." *The China Syndrome* opened on March 16, 1979, and on March 28, Unit 2 nuclear power plant on Three Mile Island near Harrisburg, Pennsylvania, suffered a partial core meltdown—mirroring almost exactly the movie's plot. The public's negative reaction to the reactor became a core issue, causing a proactive meltdown against radioactivity.

The lovable Muppet characters Bert and Ernie, from *Sesame Street,* were named after Bert, the cop, and Ernie, the taxi driver, in Frank Capra's 1946 classic *It's a Wonderful Life.*

All Aboard the SS Guppy

In the old Cap'n Crunch cereal commercials, the Cap'n's nemesis, Jean LaFoote, the "barefoot pirate," occasionally exclaimed, "Sacrebleu!" (He also said, "You can't get away with the Crunch, because the crunch always gives you away," but I digress.) So what does *sacrebleu* mean? Louis IX, who ruled France from 1226–1270, was very religious and didn't allow "taking the Lord's name in vain" in the form of swearing. In French, *dieu* means "God," and it was common for people to exclaim "Pardieu!" (by God) or "Cordieu!" (God's heart) or "Sacredieu!" (holy God). But since Louis, who was later canonized as Saint Louis, wouldn't allow swearing anymore, people adapted their language and substituted the word *dieu* with the rhyming word *bleu*, meaning, well, "blue." The words *parbleu* (by blue) and *sacrebleu* (holy blue) were born. Basically, it's the equivalent of the American "holy cow." And with that, I bid you adieu.

Dropping a Load

In January 1966, a KC-135 tanker collided with a B-52 during midair refueling, and the ensuing explosion released all four of the B-52's 20-megaton nuclear bombs over Palomares, Spain. Two of the bombs' explosive igniters detonated on impact, spreading radioactive plutonium over a large portion of the Spanish countryside. (Fortunately, no nuclear reaction took place.) The third bomb bounced off the ground and harmlessly nestled into a crater of its own making. The fourth bomb landed in the Mediterranean Sea. In order to retrieve that unexploded bomb, the U.S. Sixth Fleet, consisting of 33 ships and 3,000 men, searched for nearly three months before they could find and recover the weapon. I'm sure after they found the highly radioactive device, everyone was all aglow.

Ten-gallon hats cannot hold ten gallons of anything—
they don't even hold one gallon. They are pretty much filled
to the brim with three quarts.

Bizarre Book Titles

According to a report issued by the Book Industry Study Group, the number of books published per year is rapidly approaching 200,000. So they can't all be blockbusters—heck, they can't all even be good. Here are some examples of actual and historically bizarre book titles:

- *Animals as Criminals,* J. Brand (1896)
- *A Pictorial Book of Tongue Coating,* Anonymous (1981)
- *Fish Who Answer the Telephone,* Professor Y. P. Frolov (1937)
- *Cancer: Is the Dog the Cause?* Samuel Cort (1933)
- *The Romance of Leprosy,* E. Mackerchar (1949)
- *The Baby Jesus Touch and Feel Book,* Linda Parry and Alan Parry (1995)
- *Constipation and Civilization,* J. C. Thomson (1943)

A Healthy Constitution

The U.S. Constitution is the supreme law of the United States and one of the most famous documents in history. The framers of the U.S. Constitution must have foreseen the document they crafted as being nearly flawless—but actually a lot of the delegates at the Constitutional Convention on September 17, 1787, hated it! Compromises had to be made in order to get some members of the convention to sign; fifteen never did. They all agreed that "something is better than nothing," so they passed the Constitution with the proposal that new delegates could meet in a few years and draft a superior document. No new document was created and the Constitution as written remained. Alexander Hamilton was so unhappy with the document that in 1802 he called the Constitution "a frail and worthless fabric."

After his famous but failed midnight ride,
Paul Revere submitted a bill for his expenses in the
amount of ten pounds, four shillings.

Telegraphic Liar

The inventor of Morse code, Samuel Morse, we are told, invented the telegraph in 1844. It's true he invented Morse code, but the telegraph itself was invented in 1831 by Joseph Henry, a Princeton University professor. So why is Morse given the credit? Because Professor Henry never applied for a patent. Morse obtained Henry's sketches and papers and based his telegraph largely on the work already done by Henry. He even called the professor when he was stuck on a problem he couldn't figure out, and Henry was always willing to assist and encourage Morse. But years later, when Morse became incredibly rich and famous, he would give no acknowledgment to Henry's contribution to the creation of the telegraph—not a dot or a dash.

Wagons, Ho!

In movies about the westward expansion, we usually see settlers traveling in huge Conestoga wagons laden with family possessions and pulled by a team of horses. It's a very romantic vision of the pioneers who trekked across the United States—but, of course, it isn't true. Conestoga wagons were far too heavy, and horses were not strong enough to pull a loaded wagon over the rough terrain or for that distance. What settlers used were smaller more agile wagons called "prairie schooners" pulled by oxen or mules. Conestoga wagons are used in movies because they look better—and isn't that more important than the truth?

Dumb Statements in History

"I tell you, Wellington is a bad general, the English are bad soldiers; we will settle the matter by lunchtime."

(Napoleon Bonaparte at the Battle of Waterloo, 1815)

A Wolf in Sleak Clothing

The Society of Indecency to Naked Animals (SINA) was founded by G. Clifford Prout and Alan Abel in the 1950s. The society's goal was to clothe the millions of naked animals throughout the world, and they used such catchy slogans as "Decency today means morality tomorrow" and "A nude horse is a rude horse." Soon Prout became a familiar face on television, and on August 21, 1962, he reached the apex of exposure when the society was featured on *CBS News* with Walter Cronkite. But it was also because of this appearance that the bottom dropped out of the creature cover-up—Prout was recognized as being comedian Buck Henry. But Abel kept the hoax going a few more years by means of a SINA newsletter to the human members, who were adamant about covering animals' members. The team of Buck Henry and Alan Abel took the term *clotheshorse* to a whole different level.

❧

French poodles are not from France—
they were originally bred in Germany.

A Space All Your Own

In 1984, Stanley E. Adams, president of the Lamar Savings and Loan Association of Texas, applied for permission to open a new branch of his S&L. The attorney general's office concluded that Adams's request was far too "speculative" and rejected it outright. The savings and loan was an established business, so how speculative could creating a new branch be? In this case, it was due to the proposed location of the new branch—on the moon. Or more exactly, in the words from the actual proposal, the savings and loan would reside in "'outer space, including the Moon and other celestial bodies,' as these terms are used in the treaty of Principles Governing the Activities of States in the Exploration and Use of Outer Space, Including the Moon and Other Celestial Bodies." In 1988, Lamar Savings and Loan, along with hundreds of other S&Ls, collapsed in part of the largest theft in the history of the world, known as the Savings and Loan Scandal. No one ever saw an S&L built on the moon or anywhere in space, but people who had invested their money in S&Ls did see it sucked into a black hole.

Now We'll Have Dick Nixon to Kick Around Again

John Hockenberry, host of *Talk of the Nation*, a program on National Public Radio, announced on April 1, 1992, that Richard Nixon, in a surprise move, was running for president again. An audio clip had Nixon's voice announcing his new campaign slogan, "I didn't do anything wrong, and I won't do it again." Hockenberry then opened up the phone lines to callers, who responded with anger, shock, and outrage. Hockenberry continued covering the breaking story until the second half of the show, when he finally admitted he had been a Tricky Dick himself—the story was a practical joke. Nixon's voice had been impersonated by comedian/mimic Rich Little. Of course, a lot of people would say that Nixon's presidency was itself a joke.

Grover Cleveland was mayor of Buffalo, governor of New York State, and president of the United States— all within a span of three and a half years. He is also the only U.S. president to serve two nonconsecutive terms.

Dead on Target

In 1943, Great Britain was crafting a plan to invade Sicily but needed the Germans and Italians to think they were invading elsewhere. They needed a spy, but he had to be a stiff—and I don't mean uptight, I mean an honest to goodness dead person. They gave the dead man a new name, Major William Martin, some fictitious history, English currency, love letters, and a cryptic letter outlining an imminent invasion of either Sardinia, on the right side of Italy, or Greece, on the left. The body was tossed from a British submarine off the coast of Spain, where it soon washed ashore. The Germans believed the information was correct and removed troops to the coasts of Greece and Sardinia. That night, thousands of British soldiers parachuted onto the relatively unguarded island of Sicily. They are credited with being the crucial first line of soldiers that ultimately made the D-Day invasion possible. A dead, fictitious man played a key role in one of the most decisive battles of World War II—I guess that's truly esprit de corpse.

⚜

Tennessee Williams was born in Mississippi.

More Bizarre Books

- *The Pleasures of the Torture Chamber,* John Swain (1931)
- *Teach Yourself Alcoholism,* Meier Glatt (1975)
- *Build Your Own "Hindenburg,"* Alan Rose (1983)
- *The Bright Side of Prison Life,* Captain S. A. Swiggert (1897)
- *Children Are Wet Cement,* Ann Orlund (1981)
- *Scouts in Bondage,* Geoffrey Prout (1930)
- *Do Snakes Have Legs?* Bert Cunningham (1934)
- *How to Become a Schizophrenic,* John Modrow (1992)
- *The Day I Passed the Statue of Liberty,* Selma Reitmeir (1990)
- *Reusing Old Graves,* D. Davies and A. Shaw (1998)

Casting a Wide Internet

In the April 1994 issue of *PC Computing* magazine, John Dvorak wrote an article describing legislation going through Congress making it illegal to use the Internet while intoxicated or to communicate about sexual matters online. The bill number was 040194, which also stands for 04/01/94, or April Fools' Day; in fact, the name of the contact person was Lirpa Sloof—or *April Fools* spelled backward. The fictitious bill gave the FBI authority to wiretap anyone who "uses or abuses alcohol" while accessing the Internet. "The moniker 'Information Highway' itself seems to be responsible for SB 040194," went the article. "I know how silly this sounds, but Congress apparently thinks being drunk on a highway is bad no matter what kind of highway it is." Soon congressional phone lines were jammed with angry protests regarding the phony bill. For Senator Edward Kennedy, the hoax was as clear as the nose on his face. He had his office immediately issue a press release that denied he was a sponsor of the bill.

The titmouse is actually a bird.

Nun but the Brave

Sister Mary Luc-Gabrielle, of the Dominican Fichermont Convent in Belgium, was known for her music and, encouraged by the other nuns, recorded an album in 1963 under the name "Soeur Sourire" (or "Sister Smile"). The single from her album, "Dominique," quickly ascended to the top of the music charts, and in the United States she became known as the Singing Nun. In 1963, she won a Grammy Award for Best Gospel or Religious Recording; in 1964, she appeared on *The Ed Sullivan Show*; and in 1966, a movie called *The Singing Nun*, starring Debbie Reynolds, was released. After some soul-searching, the Dominican nun decided to kick the religious habit, changed her name back to Jeanine Deckers, and vowed to make music her full-time career. But the sound of music ended when Deckers, after years of struggling to regain her former popularity, committed suicide on March 29, 1985.

❧

The men who in 1908 wrote and composed the anthem to baseball "Take Me Out to the Ball Game," Jack Norworth and Albert von Tilzer, had never been to a baseball game.

History in the Making

One reason history is so difficult to keep straight is that people have different perceptions of events and write about them accordingly. (Some purposely manipulate the facts for alternative reasons.) Here are three examples, published on the same day, from different newspapers in Europe:

- "Latest figures show no growth in retail sales." (*Guardian*, 11/18/1986)
- "Retail spending holds up well in October." (*Daily Telegraph*, 11/18/1986)
- "October retail sales up 10%." (*Today*, 11/18/1986)

Here are two other examples published on the same date and on the same topic:

- "Industry's raw material and fuel costs rose by less than is normal at this time of year." (*The Times*, 1/13/1987)
- "Manufacturers' fuel and raw material costs jumped sharply in December." (*Financial Times*, 1/13/1987)

Precooked Fish

On the morning of February 5, 1958, a B-47 bomber collided with an F-86 fighter jet. The pilot of the F-86 bailed out safely, and his plane crashed. The B-47 was damaged but flyable. The crew was given permission to jettison the 7,600-pound, 12-foot-long thermonuclear bomb into the Atlantic Ocean off Savannah, Georgia, and that is where the bomb still is to this day. An air force investigation concluded in 2001 that the bomb was "probably harmless" if left where it was, insisting that the bomb had been used for practice and did not contain the plutonium trigger needed for a nuclear explosion. In July 2004, a group led by retired air force lieutenant colonel Derek Duke said a large object was found underwater near Savannah, possibly the nuclear bomb, as it was emitting high levels of radioactivity.

⁓❧⁓

According to the environmental group Greenpeace,
an estimated fifty nuclear warheads, most of them
from the former Soviet Union, still lie on the
bottom of the world's oceans.

Still More Bizarre Book Titles

- *New Guinea Tapeworms and Jewish Grandmothers: Tales of Parasites and People,* Robert S. Desowitz (1981)
- *Sex After Death,* B. J. Ferrell and D. E. Frey (1983)
- *How to Get Fat,* Edward Smith (1865)
- *How to Cook Husbands,* Elizabeth Strong Worthington (1899)
- *Cold Meat and How to Disguise It,* M. E. Rattray (1904)
- *Sex Life of the Foot and Shoe,* William Rossi (1977)
- *How to Be Happy Though Married,* E. J. Hardy (1885)
- *Let's Make Some Undies,* Marion Hall (1954)
- *One Hundred and Forty-one Ways of Spelling Birmingham,* William Hamper (1880)

From late July into early September, everyone cranks up the air-conditioning in anticipation of the sweltering dog days of summer. It certainly is an apropos name—because, like overheated dogs, we just want to lie around, drink a lot of cold beverages, and pant. But the dog days of summer aren't named after dogs. They're named after Sirius, the Dog Star, which prominently rises and sets with the sun during this time of year. The ancients thought the heat of Sirius combined with the heat from the sun created this doggone hot time of the year.

All the News That's Fit to Print

Earlier, I gave examples of contradictory reporting of modern events, and if we can't even get the facts straight immediately after they happen, how are we going to keep history straight? We can't. Here are more examples of newspaper articles, published on the same day, with very different viewpoints:

- "Trade Perks Up" (*Independent*, 1/29/1987)
- "Trade Deficit Worst on Record" (*Independent*, 1/29/1987)

Or how about these:

- "Growth Rate Slows in Third Quarter" (*Financial Times*, 12/20/1986)
- "Economy Grows 2%" (*Independent*, 12/20/1986)
- "Economy at 1% Growth" (*Daily Telegraph*, 12/20/1986)
- "Economy Well Short at Only 0.3%" (*Guardian*, 12/20/1986)
- "A Growing Economy" (*Today*, 12/20/1986)

Despite its name, the century plant does not bloom every hundred years. In fact, in favorable climates, it could be called the "decade plant" because it usually blooms every five to ten years. The century plant has been known, however, to take as long as sixty years to bloom.

Getting Down to Brass Tacks

At the same time explorer Samuel Wallis discovered the Tahitian Islands in June 1767, his crewmen discovered the native women would trade sex for iron nails. The Tahitians found many uses for iron nails, and they soon became more precious than silver or gold. Soon a very precarious condition evolved: On the one hand, you had beautiful exotic women willing to "do anything" for iron nails, and on the other hand, you had lonely, bored sailors with nothing to do but figure out how to get their hands on iron nails—thereby getting their hands on the beautiful exotic women. And at the heart of the dilemma was the HMS *Dolphin*—a wooden ship held together by iron nails. Captain Wallis was forced to forbid the trade. "It was soon found that all the belaying cleats had been ripped off," wrote the captain in his log, "and that there was scarcely one of the hammock nails left." The nail crisis came to a head when a Mr. Pinckney's robust transactions led to the collapse of the mainsail. I'm not sure about this, but it's possible this is where "nailing" or "getting nailed" became synonymous with sex.

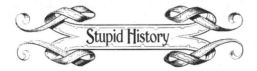

Myth

The forbidden fruit said to be plucked from the Tree of Knowledge of Good and Evil and eaten by Adam and Eve was an apple.

Truth

Not sure. The Bible references only the "fruit of the tree" (Genesis 3:3) and names no particular fruit. In Christianity, the fruit is usually portrayed as an apple, but in Judaism, it is thought to be a fig, grapes, a citron, or wheat.

First in Our Hearts, Maybe...

Here's something about the presidents we all know is correct: George Washington was the first president of the United States. Nope. Think about it: The original thirteen colonies of the United States claimed their independence from England through the Declaration of Independence signed in 1776. Okay. Now, George Washington wasn't elected president of the United States until 1789. That means there is a gap of thirteen years between the founding of our nation and the election of the first president. Who ran the country during those first thirteen years? John Hanson, that's who. John Hanson was elected "President of the United States in Congress Assembled" by a unanimous vote of Congress on November 5, 1781. He served for one year.

Hanson was then followed by Elias Boudinot, the second president of the United States; Thomas Mifflin, the third president; Richard Henry Lee, the fourth; Nathan Gorman, the fifth; Arthur St. Claire, the sixth; and Cyrus Griffin, the seventh. And coming in at number eight is good old George Washington.

One overlooked fact about the Boston
Tea Party of December 16, 1773, is that the
colonists, dressed as Indians, inadvertently
chose low tide to throw the party—
and the tea—overboard. What happened
was that the nearly 350 crates of tea piled up
in the shallow water, and the partygoers had
to jump overboard and smash open the crates
to make sure the tea was ruined.

A Pachyderm of Lies

An article in the April 1984 edition of *Technology Review* titled "Retrobreeding the Woolly Mammoth" described an effort by Soviet scientists to bring the woolly mammoth back from extinction. The article explained that DNA, taken from a woolly mammoth found frozen in the Siberian ice, was injected into living elephant cells. The elephant served as a surrogate mother for the hybrid cells, which gestated full-term, producing the first "mammontelephas." The heads of the project were reported as being one Dr. Sverbighooze Nikhiphorovich Yasmilov of the University of Irkutsk and a Dr. James Creak of MIT. But the story of the newly created woolly mammoth was nothing but a shaggy dog story concocted as an April Fools' joke by Diana Ben-Aaron. However, before the story became known as a hoax, it was widely reported in the mainstream media as a real mammoth scientific breakthrough. Another example of the news media getting the woolly pulled over their eyes.

❧

The gray whale is actually black.

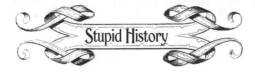

A Token of Their Appreciation

In October 1971, the Arbeia Roman Fort and Museum in South Shields, England, was proudly displaying an exhibition of Roman artifacts found nearby. (The museum is located near the end of Hadrian's Wall, built by the Romans around A.D. 160.) One case contained a Roman sesterce coin, identified by museum experts as having been minted sometime between A.D. 135 and A.D. 138.

But one visitor, nine-year-old Fiona Gordon, claimed to have seen similar coins much later than that—given out as a token by a local soda bottler. She pointed out the soda bottler's trademark on the reverse of the coin. The *R* museum officials had originally taken to mean "Roman" actually stood for the soft drink manufacturer—Robinson's. The realization they had been displaying a fake Roman coin made the curators feel like glutei maximi.

Saying someone is "attracted like a moth to a flame" doesn't really have the meaning we normally think. Moths aren't actually attracted to light, and the only reason they fly straight into bright lights is because it confuses their navigation system. Moths use light rays from the moon and sun as a guide, constantly checking their position against the angle of the light rays, but when the source of the light is too close, it basically overrides this delicate balance, and the moth flutters closer and closer to the light.

Holmes Is Where the Heart Is

The fictional detective Sherlock Holmes is known for his deductive reasoning, his calabash pipe, his deerstalker hat, and his catchphrase, "Elementary, my dear Watson." But even fictional characters aren't safe from being fictionalized. Case in point, my dear reader: Between 1887 and 1927, British writer Sir Arthur Conan Doyle published four novels and fifty-six short stories about the celebrated detective and his physician-sidekick, Dr. John H. Watson—and not once is a calabash pipe, a deerstalker hat, or the phrase "Elementary, my dear Watson" mentioned. So why are these things attributed to him? Over the years, actors portraying the character of Sherlock Holmes have been responsible for embellishing his dress and his speech. Side note: Holmes was a Victorian and wouldn't have made the fashion faux pas of wearing a deerstalker hat (country apparel) in the city—and I've just proven that I'm a dork.

Charles Dickens's immortal character Ebenezer Scrooge in *A Christmas Carol* blurts out, "Bah, humbug!" when referring to Christmas. It sounds nasty, but what does it mean? The word *humbug* is an archaic term meaning "hoax," "jest," or "fraud."

I've Heard of Ham-Fisted Before, But . . .

The British newspaper the *Daily Mail* reported in April 2000 that Esporta Health Clubs had designed a new line of socks to help people lose weight. Named FatSox, these revolutionary socks, which employed the patented nylon polymer FloraAstraTetrazine, reportedly sucked "excess lipids from the body through the sweat." Once FatSox were soaked with perspiration, said inventor Professor Frank Ellis Elgood, the wearer simply removed the socks and washed them—removing dirt, grime, smell, and more importantly, fat. The article was reported through worldwide media outlets, and editors who believed this April Fools' story should wear FatSox instead of hats to decrease the size of their fat heads.

American patriot Nathan Hale's last words
were not "I only regret that I have but one life to lose for my
country." The recently discovered diary of Captain Frederick
MacKenzie, who was present at the hanging on September 22, 1776,
reported that Hale's last words were "It is the duty of every good
officer to obey any orders given him by his commander-in-chief."
Not nearly as emotional as the ones we're used to—which in all
probability were paraphrased from Joseph Addison's 1713 drama
Cato, wherein a character bemoans, "What pity is it that we can die
but once to serve our country!"

Just Wing It

A plane with one wing is called a *monoplane,* a plane with two wings is called a *biplane,* and a plane with three wings is called a *triplane.* But what do you call a plane with nine wings? Count Giovanni Caproni's Ca.60 Transaereo flying boat. Caproni was an Italian nobleman who owned Società Italiana Caproni, Milano—an airplane factory that built bombers for the Allied Forces during World War I and World War II. Caproni dreamed of building a 100-passenger transatlantic airliner that could fly from Italy to New York. Most people thought he could do this only "on a wing and a prayer"—so he hedged his bet and made a plane with nine wings. On March 4, 1921, his test pilot fired up the engines, taxied across Lake Maggiore, took off, and obtained an altitude of about sixty feet. Then for some reason (possibly because it was an engineering monstrosity), the plane suddenly nosedived, disintegrated in midair, and slammed into the lake. The pilot wasn't hurt, but Caproni's image as an aircraft designer was.

❧

The style of wood board called the 2-by-4 does not measure 2 by 4 inches, but $1\frac{3}{4}$ inches by $3\frac{1}{2}$ inches. The board originally measures 2 by 4 inches before planing, smoothing, and drying.

Jiminy Cricket, That's a Big Grasshopper

On September 9, 1937, the front-page headline of the *Tomah (Wisconsin) Monitor-Herald* warned people: "Giant Grasshoppers Invade Butts Orchard East of City." The article explained that grasshoppers had eaten special plant food used on an apple orchard belonging to farmer A. L. Butts and had quickly grown to three feet in length. Accompanying the article were photographs of shotgun-toting hunters tracking down the mutant insects as well as a picture of Farmer Butts holding up a dead grasshopper like a prize fish. The citizens of the town became jumpy and nearly hysterical at the thought of enormous grasshoppers bouncing through the town, destroying their crops, frightening the livestock, and generally wreaking havoc. The article, of course, was a hoax, and *Monitor-Herald* publisher, B. J. Fuller, along with Farmer Butts (yes, there was an actual Farmer Butts), confessed to making the townsfolk the butt of their elaborate, and pesky, joke.

What does a "corny" joke have to do with corn?
I stalked down a kernel of an answer. Corn seed
catalogs during the late nineteenth and early
twentieth centuries made for some pretty boring
reading. So the publishers started including very
obvious, silly, or just plain stupid jokes to keep their
readers' attention. The jokes became popular, and that
particular type of humor was called a "corn catalog
joke," which was shortened to just plain "corny."

Really in the Rough

The Republic of Benin, a small nation in West Africa, doesn't have a golf course, but a technicality like that never gets in the way of a true duffer like Mathieu Boya. Benin has five airfields within its borders, but only one has a paved runway; it was here at the Benin Air Base (Force Aerienne Populaire de Benin) where Boya routinely practiced driving golf balls. Boya wasn't playing a round of golf that day in 1987, but he did hit a birdie—actually, he struck a hapless passing seagull. The unconscious gull fell into the open cockpit of a French-built Mirage III fighter taxiing the runway and landed on the pilot's lap. The bird regained consciousness and began flapping wildly, which startled the pilot, who lost control of the plane and crashed it into the four other Mirage fighter jets sitting on the tarmac. The pilot was okay, and the gull flew out of the cockpit before impact, but all five jets, the entire fighter defense force of the Benin nation, were completely destroyed. So the errant ball flew into the flying bird who landed on the flyboy and ended the flights of the Benin Air Force.

Cutting Off Your Circulation

Unhappy with the depth of reporting in English newspapers, Lionel Burleigh decided to publish his own paper in 1965 called the *Commonwealth Sentinel*. Burleigh worked diligently for weeks writing articles, promoting the newspaper on billboards, selling advertising space, and printing up 50,000 copies to make the first edition a success. On February 6, after the newspaper had left the printers, an exhausted Burleigh was resting in his hotel room when he was interrupted by a call from the London constabulary. "Have you anything to do with the *Commonwealth Sentinel*?" the officer asked. "Because there are 50,000 on the outside entrance to Brown's Hotel and they're blocking Albemarle Street." With the hundreds of details to attend to when publishing a newspaper, Burleigh had forgotten one: He never got a distributor. Britain's "most fearless paper" folded the following day.

Pope John XXI, who served as pope for only eight months, added a new wing to his palace at Viterbo, Italy. The workmanship was shoddy, and on May 12, 1277, while the pope lay sleeping, part of the roof fell in, and he was seriously injured. John XXI became just another name and number on the long list of popes after he succumbed to his wounds and died eight days later.

X-ing Out Christmas

You would think the Puritans, who were known for their religious fervor, must have loved Christmas—but they didn't. In fact, a law was passed in 1659 outlawing the celebration of Christmas. A five-shilling fine was levied against anyone "found observing, by abstinence from labor, feasting or any other way, any such days as Christmas day." They considered Christmas "an extreme forgetfulness of Christ, by giving liberty to carnal and sensual delights." For being Puritans, they sure talked about sex a lot, didn't they?

It's not likely that any of the "traditional" Thanksgiving foods were served by the Pilgrims in 1621. It's true they had a feast, but it was not called a feast of "thanksgiving," as that implied to the devoutly religious colonists a day of fasting and prayer. It is possible they had turkey, but only the term *fowl* is used. It is known that the Indians brought five deer for the feast and it lasted for three days and was a one-time occurrence—not the beginning of a tradition. But one thing is sure—there was no apple pie. Apples are not native to North America—they came from Europe and West Asia.

Heavy Is the Head That Wears the Crown

When King Charles II fell ill on the morning of February 2, 1685, a team of six doctors were immediately at his side—and it might have been the worst thing to ever happen to him. The following are some of the procedures used on the king:

- They let (drained) sixteen ounces of blood.
- In order to "stimulate the system," they applied heated cups to the skin that formed large round blisters.
- They let eight more ounces of blood.
- They induced vomiting to cleanse his stomach, gave him an enema to purify his bowels, and made him swallow a purgative to evacuate his intestines.

This type of torturous treatment continued for four days. More bleedings, more blistering, more purging, more vomiting, more enemas, a concoction made from pigeon droppings, a cure of "40 drops of extract of human skull" of a man who had met a violent death, a force-feeding of the gallstone of a goat, and finally, "extracts of all the herbs and animals of the kingdom." The result? The king died. In comparison, dealing with an HMO sounds pretty good.

If We Took the Bones Out, It Wouldn't Be Crunchy

If the phrase "You are what you eat" is true, people who consumed a particular brand of peanut butter in 1972 must be pooped all the time. That year, the Oregon Health Department revealed that the chunks in Hoody's Chunky Style Peanut Butter were not peanuts but rat droppings. Hoody executives were sentenced to ten days in prison for health violations and were hopefully fed peanut butter sandwiches. To ensure better quality control in the future, the U.S. Food and Drug Administration issued strict new guidelines on the amount of "allowable" foreign matter in packaged foods. They include:

- No more than 50 insect fragments or 2 rodent hairs per 100 grams of peanut butter
- No more than 10 fruit fly eggs in 100 grams of tomato juice
- No more than 150 insect fragments in an 8-ounce chocolate bar

⁂

A research study conducted by Ohio University in December 2005 reported that Americans unintentionally eat one to two pounds of insect parts per year. The study didn't say, however, how many insects are eaten intentionally.

Deadly Gases Found on Uranus

In 1996, AOL's five million subscribers were met with more than the familiar "You've got mail"—they were also informed that a "government source reveals signs of life on Jupiter." Statements from a planetary biologist supported the claim, and Ted Leonsis, AOL's vice chairman, stated that his company possessed documents proving the government was hiding the facts about life on Jupiter. The story quickly generated over 1,300 messages on AOL as well as hundreds of calls to NASA and the Jet Propulsion Laboratory in Pasadena, California. It turned out to be AOL's little joke . . . sort of like their customer support.

Myth
Alan Shepard coined the phrase "A-OK" during his first space flight in the *Freedom 7* spacecraft on May 5, 1961.

Truth
No. Colonel "Shorty" Powers, the "voice of mission control" and NASA's public affairs officer at the time, introduced the phrase but attributed it to Shepard, hoping it would catch on.

Line, Please!

Fortunately, as time goes by, fewer and fewer untalented impersonators attempt to do a takeoff of James Cagney. But if you're ever unlucky enough to hear one, you will inevitably hear the line "You dirty rat!" (along with the shrugged shoulders and the overbite). But Cagney, famous for his portrayal of gangsters in more than seventy movies, never said this line. The closest he ever got was in the 1932 film *Taxi!,* in which Cagney delivered the line "Come out and take it, you dirty, yellow-bellied rat, or I'll give it to you through the door!"

✦

In 1928 in Altendorf, Germany, a high wind caused a farmer's windmill to spin so quickly that it caused a tremendous amount of heat to be generated through friction, which caused the windmill to catch on fire and burn to the ground.

In Sickness and in Health— for Richer or for Poorer

Robert Meier watched as his comatose girlfriend's vital signs got weaker and weaker and made the decision to marry her before she died. People in the hospital thought it was a romantic gesture as Meier and his girlfriend became husband and wife only hours before her death. But later, in July 1996, Meier was arrested in Tampa, Florida, for using his dead wife's credit card to rack up more than $20,000 in expenses. Did Meier claim to be distraught over his wife's passing and driven by depression to go on a shopping spree? No—he blamed her dog. According to police records, "[Meir] said the dog told him she [his wife] would want him to have a better life, so it would be okay to use her credit cards." It makes sense that Meier would speak to a dog—it sounds like he was a real son-of-a-bitch.

Dumb Statements in History

"If excessive smoking actually plays a role in the production of lung cancer, it seems to be a minor one."
(The National Cancer Institute, 1954)

Are the Noises in My Head Bothering You?

At one time or another, we've all been accused of not acting like ourselves. But Cathleen Byers, former manager of the Oregon Urban Rural Credit Union, used this as a legal argument in February 1997, after she was arrested for embezzlement. Byers confessed to stealing $630,000 over six years but claimed she was innocent because it wasn't really her—it was one of her other personalities. Byers allegedly suffered from multiple personality disorder, so Ava, Joy, Elizabeth, Tillie, Claudia, C. J., Katy, Roman, Cookie, Mariah, Frogger, Chrissy, or Colleen must have been embezzling all that time without her knowledge. An expert testified that Byers's other personalities didn't know right from wrong, and Byers's right personality didn't know what her wrong personality was doing. The judge rightly didn't believe Byers was wrongly accused, stating: "[Byers] should have been clued in by the new house and the luxury cars."

How Much Are the One-Cent Stamps?

If said with enough authority, a great number of people won't question what they read or hear and then will pass the erroneous information on to others. Here's an example of an actual ad from the U.S. Postal Service from 1996, defending its policy to raise the price of stamps:

> *In 1940, a one-pound loaf of bread cost 8 cents, and in 1995 cost 79 cents; a half-gallon of milk went from 25 cents to $1.43 in the same period; and a first-class postage stamp went from 3 cents to 32 cents. Which, bottom line, means that first-class postage stamps remain well below the rate of inflation.*

Sounds great, doesn't it? But do the math: These examples actually prove the price of stamps rose 9 percent faster than the price of bread and 105 percent faster than the price of milk. But the post office is a monopoly, and their express priority is selling stamps and services, even if that means stretching the envelope on honesty.

❧

According to the Mormon religion, anyone who isn't Mormon is called a Gentile—anyone. So in essence, in Utah, even Jews are considered Gentiles.

One More Time from the Top

Lieutenant General Nathan Bedford Forrest was leading his Confederate troops to Alabama in late September 1864 to attack the Union post located in Athens. But there was an overwhelming problem: The post was well manned and heavily fortified. The general knew he was greatly outnumbered, and he knew Union reinforcements were on the way, but he had a plan. He sent a message to Union commander Colonel Wallace Campbell requesting a personal meeting. Campbell agreed to the meeting, and on September 24, 1864, Forrest escorted Campbell on a tour of his Confederate troops. Campbell took the opportunity to secretly count the number of soldiers and artillery he saw surrounding his fort. But what Campbell didn't count on was that Forrest had ordered his men, after being inspected and tallied, to pack up their belongings and quietly move to the back of the line to be counted again. After counting continuous counterfeit Confederates, Campbell returned to his fort, believing he was heavily outnumbered, and surrendered without a fight.

A Cramped Expression

Some common phrases we take for granted don't make a lot of sense unless you know the context in which they were created. Like the term *charley horse*. We know what a charley horse is—it's a muscle cramp. But how did it get such a weird name? Here's the answer: In 1640, Charles I of England expanded the London police force. The nickname "Charley" was given to new recruits in mock honor of the person responsible for their hiring, Charles I. The new recruits soon discovered there wasn't enough money to supply them with horses—so they were forced to patrol on foot. After a full day of walking the beat, the new officers joked that their sore feet and legs were the result of riding "Charley's horse."

Rice paper is not made from rice, but from the *pith*, the spongy, fibrous tissue, of an evergreen shrub called the tetrapanax.

Pennies from Heaven

"Every cloud has a silver lining," but residents of the Gorki region of the former USSR had the silver lining rain down on them when several thousand rubles' worth of silver coins fell from the sky on June 17, 1940. Authorities offered the official explanation that a landslide had uncovered a hidden treasure that was carried away by a passing tornado and dropped on Gorki. Doubt was shed on this theory, as the coins were the only thing that rained down—there was no debris.

French fries didn't come from France—but they are fried. The origin of French fries is nineteenth-century Belgium, where *patates frites* (fried potatoes) were served on the street in paper cones. The *French* in French fries originally referred not to the country of origin, but to the way the food was prepared.

Stop Calling Me a Weenie Dog!

If you've ever owned a pet, you know the helpless feeling of not being able to explain to them when something is wrong—especially if it involves the embarrassing topic of sexual frustration. So veterinarians and pet owners alike were pleased when an article came out in *The Independent* in 2000 reporting on Feralmone, a Viagra-like pill that could help pets overcome their feelings of inadequacy. "It's not unknown for a guinea pig to sit in its cage thinking, 'I haven't had sex for months. Am I so unattractive?'" the article read. Unfortunately, the article was a joke—forcing dogs all around the world to once again resort to humping table legs.

Myth
The Bible says, "Pride goeth before a fall."

Truth
No. What Proverbs 16:18 says is, "Pride goeth before destruction, and an haughty spirit before a fall."

Colonel Bat Guano ... If That Is Your Real Name

Countries have invaded other countries for centuries in order to increase their size or to lay claim to natural resources like gold, silver, copper, and oil. But in 1865, the United States passed an act to acquire by "peaceable possession" any uninhabited, unclaimed island, mainly in the South Pacific, for the sole purpose of taking their crap. The Guano Act of 1865 authorized the United States to occupy these islands to mine guano (bird droppings), which is rich in nitrogen and phosphorus and highly valued as a fertilizer. The United States claimed nearly 100 islands under the act and still owns 6 or so today. As to the amount of crap the government still has—that's for you to decide.

Lincoln's Résumé

Abraham Lincoln was a great president and a great leader, so he must have developed his greatness from his former positions . . . but most of his former positions were flops:

- He ran for the Illinois state legislature in 1832 and lost—he also lost his job.
- In 1833, his grocery business failed. (It took him fifteen years to pay off the debt.)
- He was elected to the state legislature in 1834, but he lost races for Illinois house speaker in 1836 and 1838.
- In 1843, he ran for Congress and lost.
- He was elected to Congress in 1846 but lost his renomination bid in 1848.
- In 1849, he lost the race for land officer.
- He lost the U.S. Senate race in 1854 and, in 1856, was defeated for the nomination for vice president.
- In 1858, he again lost his bid for U.S. Senate.
- In 1860, he was elected president and then reelected in 1864 (and we all know how well that worked out for him).

This Is My Good Friend, Harvey

In 1726, an English maid, Mary Toft, reported to the authorities that she had been accosted and molested by a six-foot rabbit. Some of the townsfolk were skeptical, and some actually believed her, ordering their wives and daughters to stay inside at night and, of course, not to open the door to any six-foot rabbits. Five months after the rabbit rape, Mary collapsed in a field and was declared pregnant by a local doctor. A little over a month later, Mary gave birth, and the baby looked just like its father—a rabbit. Over the next few days, Mary gave birth to seven more rabbits, all of them dead. News of the bunny babies reached King George I, and he sent two of England's finest physicians to investigate. The doctors performed various tests on the dead rabbits and amazingly declared the births genuine. Under the direction of a third expert, Mary was moved to a London hospital and put under round-the-clock surveillance. During that time, Mary didn't move a hare. A gardener confessed to supplying Mary and her husband with baby rabbits, and Mary finally admitted the ruse. She told authorities the motivation behind the hoax was her husband had lost his job and they were hoping for a pension from the king. The king did give Mary something—a prison term for fraud. I guess the king was angry about the deception—you could say he was hopping mad.

❧

Guinea pigs are not pigs, and they are not from Guinea
(West Africa). They are rodents native to the Andean region
of South America.

Animal Sounds

"Music hath charms to soothe the savage beast" gives the impression that if you played a violin for a charging bull, it would stop in its tracks and softly sway to the music. I wouldn't suggest doing that because the above-mentioned statement is misquoted. What British playwright William Congreve actually wrote in his play *The Mourning Bride* (1697) is "Music hath charms to soothe a savage breast." Of course, if a "savage breast" is charging you, I suggest you've seen too many Woody Allen movies.

Raggin' on Wagons

A much-beloved image of the Old West is that of wagon trains traveling in straight, single-file lines across the prairies. Wagon trains, whenever possible, traveled side-by-side, up to ten miles wide, to avoid the billowing clouds of dust as well as the furrows, ruts, and potholes of previous travelers. If they had in fact traveled single-file, every wagon behind the lead would not only eat their dust, they would also wear it and have it clog their nostrils and cake over their eyes.

The term *cowboy* was not created in the Wild West. The Spanish created what we consider the cowboy tradition in the sixteenth century with the *vaquero* (Spanish for "cowboy"). In the United States, the word *cowboy* originally referred to a member of a team that rustled cows in New York in the 1800s.

When Walter Met Elizabeth

The scene: Queen Elizabeth I walks down a London street followed by her entourage and stops in front of a puddle of mud—suddenly Sir Walter Raleigh breaks through the crowd and drapes his cloak over the puddle so the queen can walk on unmuddied. It's a scene that's been duplicated and parodied in theater and films for decades, but usually one small detail is overlooked—it never happened. This romantic story is the invention of Thomas Fuller, a seventeenth-century historian, who embellished otherwise boring historical stories or, in this case, made them up altogether. In 1821, Sir Walter Scott elaborated on the falsehood with an exchange between the two famous sixteenth-century personalities: Raleigh says admirably he will never have his cloak cleaned, to which the queen graciously offers him a tailor-made suit for his gallant actions. Very sweet, very poignant, very much made up.

❧

Emily Dickinson wrote 1,789 poems in her lifetime (1830–1886). Seven were published—all anonymously and probably without her knowledge.

But, Dad, Everybody's Wearing Them

Three teenage girls in Tokyo became fatally ill, and their deaths were blamed on a silk kimono possessed by evil demons (not the butler this time). In February 1657, a priest was summoned by the girls' fathers to see if he could perform an exorcism on the garment. At the cleansing ceremony (or the dry-cleaning ceremony), the fathers of the young victims watched as the priest reverently took a torch and, while deep in prayer, set the cloth aflame. As if on cue, a strong wind blew the kimono to the floor, catching the house on fire. The wind fanned the flames of the burning house, and soon fire engulfed the wooden dwellings throughout the city of Tokyo. Before it was contained, the notorious "Long-Sleeved Kimono Fire" (*Furisode-kaji*) incinerated three quarters of the city and took the lives of more than 100,000 people. Things could have been worse—the noise of the destruction could have awoken Godzilla!

Farting contests were held in ancient Japan, with prizes awarded for loudness and duration. And in the classic "He who does not know his history is bound to repeat it" category, farting contests are back in vogue in Japan (just check out YouTube.com).

Pressing His Luck

Johannes Gutenberg (1398–1468) is credited not only with inventing a printing press with movable type but also with ushering in the Renaissance period in Europe. In 1447, Gutenberg borrowed 800 guilders from his partner, Johann Fust, and along with Fust's son-in-law, Peter Schöffer, established his printing business with the intention of printing the Bible and quickly paying back his debt. But things didn't work out for Gutenberg, and his first Bible didn't come out until 1455—and by then, he was 2,000 guilders in debt. Fust took Gutenberg to court, where the judge declared him bankrupt and threw the book at him by awarding control of the types and plates used in his Bible, plus the printing equipment, to Fust. Fust-Schöffer printed the first book that included the printer's name (their names) and date and explained the mechanical process by which it had been produced, but it made no mention of Gutenberg. Although Gutenberg never made a penny from his invention or received any fame during his lifetime, he is bound forever in the pages of history as one of the most influential inventors of all time.

Fun with Racist Stereotypes

Gypsies are portrayed as a band of nomads who travel around in wagons and are usually considered unscrupulous. Gosh, where to start with this one. First of all, there is no such thing as a Gypsy. The people referred to as Gypsies are actually the Roma people (singular, Rom), who originate from northern India. *Gypsy* is just a designation put on them by the *gadje* (that means "barbarian," and anyone who isn't a Rom is a *gadje*). In any event, the term *Gypsy* is inaccurate—it comes from the Greek word *aigyptoi* in the erroneous belief that the Roma are natives of Egypt. (Gypsy, Egypt—see?) And what about Gypsies, tramps, and thieves (with a nod to Cher)? It is from this racist image that we get the words *gyp* and *gypped*, meaning "cheat."

Frédéric Chopin's "Minute Waltz" was not intended to be played in a minute, and the normal rendition time is one and a half to two minutes. Chopin had meant for the word *minute* to mean "small," not as a sixtieth part of an hour.

More Fun with Racist Stereotypes

In a horrible twist of fate, the Roma are technically classified as Aryan, but not the blond-haired, blue-eyed "Aryan race" Adolf Hitler envisioned. *Aryan* comes from the Sanskrit *arya*, which historically refers to the people of northern India—the Roma. Hitler absolutely hated the fact that Roma were the true Aryans and not his Aryan/ Nordic "master race." In fact, other than Jews, the Roma were the only racial group specifically targeted for extermination by the Nazis. It is estimated that between 200,000 and 500,000 Roma died in German concentration camps. So a Gypsy isn't someone with a nomadic, fun-loving, free-spirited lifestyle, but a race of persecuted people referred to by a derogatory name. Talk about getting gypped!

Rain Forest Go Away, Come Again Some Other Day

During a trip to Costa Rica in the spring of 1996, President Bill Clinton stopped off at the Braulio Carrillo National Park— a government-protected rain forest—to give a speech about environmental protection and preservation. His address included the line "We destroy these resources at our own peril." Too bad Bill's staff didn't agree. Clinton's people thought the speaking platform was too far from the road, especially since the president was on crutches at the time. They decided to bulldoze, level, and asphalt a 350-foot path for him— right through the rain forest. Later, a White House staffer tried to put a good spin on it: "The Costa Ricans were eager to pave the walkway for the president. They seemed to understand how important a photo op this was for us." Sounds like an example of not being able to see the trees for the forest. Any more photo ops like this, and we won't be able to see the trees *or* the forest.

The Final Edition of Bizarre Book Titles

In case you're looking for more unique books to fill your shelves, here's my final "best of the worst" list of book titles:

- *Games You Can Play with Your Pussy,* Ira Alterman (1885)
- *Preserving Dick,* Mary D. R. Boyd (1867)
- *How to Avoid Huge Ships,* John W. Trimmer (1993)
- *Unmentionable Cuisine,* Calvin W. Schwabe (1979)
- *Nasal Maintenance: Nursing Your Nose Through Troubled Times,* William Alan Stuart (1983)
- *Old Age: Its Cause and Prevention,* Sanford Bennett (1912)

The Swanee River, immortalized by Stephen Foster in his song "The Old Folks at Home" and by Irving Caesar and George Gershwin in "Swanee," doesn't exist—it never existed. Foster's original lyrics in 1851 experimented with the Yazoo River and the Pee Dee River and settled on the Suwannee River—but shortened the spelling to rhyme. Caesar and Gershwin reused the popular name in their 1919 song, and it was made world famous by singer Al Jolson.

The Spirits of the Republic

The fifty-five delegates who attended the Constitutional Convention from May 25 to September 17, 1787, had more on their minds than creating a new form of government—they were also there to party! One receipt dated two days before the official signing of the U.S. Constitution listed, among other items, 156 bottles of liquor. Alexander Hamilton, one of the main framers of the Constitution, was under doctor's orders to consume no more than "three glasses of wine" per day, and the fact that this regimen was considered moderate says a lot about the drinking habits of our forefathers or fifth fathers. To be able to drink that much and still have the wherewithal to formulate a new government means our Founding Fathers had a pretty strong constitution.

An American missionary in Japan invented the rickshaw around 1869 to transport his invalid wife through the streets of Yokohama. And just in case you're wondering, his name was not Rick Shaw—it was Jonathan Scobie.

Our Way or Ye Olde Highway

When we think of the Puritans, we usually think of wholesome, God-fearing, uptight people in black clothes with buckles on their hats. But were the Puritans "puritanical"? They left Europe because of religious intolerance, but once in Massachusetts, they denied their own settlers any religious freedoms of their own. In fact, religious dissenters were expelled from the colony. They weren't big fans of democracy, either—the first governor of the Massachusetts Bay Colony, John Winthrop, described democracy as "the meanest and worst of all forms of government." *Justice* to the Puritans meant "just us."

The Puritan Penal Code

"Ralph Earle, for drawing his wife in an vnciuell [uncivil] manner on the snow, is fined twenty shillings."
(From the General Court of the Plymouth Colony, October 5, 1663)

Caesar or Seize Him?

Julius Caesar, dictator of the Roman Republic (later the Roman Empire), was one of the most influential and powerful men in world history. He was a great military strategist and political leader who expanded the territory of the Roman Republic all the way to the Atlantic Ocean. With all these credentials, why was Caesar's nickname "the Queen of Bithynia"? I'll tell you. In 80 B.C., young Julius Caesar was an ambassador to King Nicomedes IV in Bithynia, a Roman province in Asia Minor, and reportedly had a fling with the king. Most of the writers of the time mention the alleged affair, and Mark Antony even charged that Caesar's adopted son, Octavian (Emperor Julius Caesar Octavianus), earned his adoption through sexual favors. Was Caesar really in love with Cleopatra, or was he just in denial?

Dumb Statements in History

"Rail travel at high speed is not possible, because passengers, unable to breathe, would die of asphyxiation."
(Dr. Dionysus Lardener, 1845)

An Unusual Stock Exchange

In Boston, Massachusetts, in 1634, a carpenter named Edward Palmer was commissioned by the town's elders to build the first wooden stocks intended for public punishment. After completing the work, Palmer submitted his bill for one pound, thirteen shillings, and seven pence, which nearly blew the buckles off the elders' shoes. Puritan officials felt the price was so high as to be considered extortion and voted to punish Palmer. He was fined five pounds and also ordered to "be sett an houre in the stocks," becoming the first victim of his handiwork. A classic example of someone taking stock of himself.

Myth

The United States of America is made up of fifty states.

Truth

Technically, no. There are only forty-six states in the United States—Kentucky, Massachusetts, Pennsylvania, and Virginia are commonwealths.

Where's the Lock Box?

In October 1937, the stock market crashed again—almost as drastically as in October 1929. The reason? In 1936, Social Security taxes were withheld from paychecks for the first time. Consumer spending dropped because people had less of their own money, the economy shrank, and unemployment shot up to 22 percent. Social Security was social (or socialism), but there was little security, because the money skimmed off people's paychecks didn't reenter the economy until January 31, 1940, when the first Social Security check was issued. A woman named Ida Mae Fuller, who had been in the system only two years and had paid in a total of $22, was the first recipient. Ida Mae lived to be 100 and ended up collecting $22,000 in Social Security benefits. And they say people don't fall for pyramid schemes anymore.

Riptides aren't tides, they are actually currents.

The Circle of Lies

A common safety rule these days, if your clothes catch on fire, is to stop, drop, and roll. But a safety rule for the pioneers of the Westward expansion was, if Indians attack, circle your wagons. Stop, drop, and roll could save your life, but circling can kill you. Can you imagine the time, labor, and logistics that would go into circling even a few wagons? Accomplishing this task would be a load off the pioneers' minds—but before it could ever happen, the Indians would have taken a load off the pioneers' minds by scalping them. Circling the wagons was an invention of Hollywood filmmakers who liked the way it looked on film. Some wagon trains did form a circle when they stopped for the night, but not to protect themselves against attack—they did it to create a makeshift corral to contain the animals.

August 8, 1945, two days after the
U.S. Army Air Force dropped the nuclear
bomb "Little Boy" on Hiroshima and one
day after "Fat Boy" devastated Nagasaki,
the Soviet Union declared war on Japan.
By doing this, the Soviets were able to
partake of the spoils of the Pacific war
without actually having to fight in it.

Cherries Jubilee

You've probably never heard of them before, but in their heyday, they were a staggeringly popular act: the Cherry Sisters (and no, they weren't strippers). The sisters' popularity didn't grow out of their talent; in fact, just the opposite, they were billed as "America's Worst Act." And people in the late 1800s flocked to hear them warble and clump around the stage—no one was disappointed at the horrific spectacle of the Cherry Sisters. The sisters went along with the billing as "America's Worst Act" and were under the delusion they were actually popular for their act and that the billing was just a publicity stunt. After a show at Hammerstein's Theater in New York in 1896, a reviewer compared their singing to "the wailings of damned souls." But when the review was reprinted in their hometown, Des Moines, Iowa, newspaper, the sisters sued for libel. During the trial, the Cherry Sisters were asked to perform their musical act for the court—they did . . . and they lost their case. From the Cherry case stems the protection of "fair comment and criticism" as part of libel law. The verdict popped the Cherry Sisters' spirit, and they went from Wild Cherries to Sour Cherries as fast as you can say Bing.

Shhhh, Don't Tell Anybody We're Here

On April 14, 1865, one of President Abraham Lincoln's last acts before retiring for the evening was establishing the Secret Service (originally for the purpose of preventing counterfeiting of currency). Later that night, John Wilkes Booth assassinated the relatively unguarded Lincoln at Ford's Theatre. Congress soon debated adding presidential protection to the duties performed by the Secret Service, but like most things in Congress, they only thought about it, they didn't actually do anything. Finally in 1894, the Secret Service was commissioned to begin informal, part-time protection of President Grover Cleveland. This was a full twenty-nine years after the assassination of Lincoln and thirteen years after the assassination of President James Garfield. I guess the Secret Service's services were secret a little too long.

Drats, Foiled Again!

Since they first appeared in the 1860s, cigarettes have caused a lot of harm, but one good thing has come out of the manufacturing of cigarettes—aluminum foil. Richard S. Reynolds (the nephew of tobacco king R. J. Reynolds) was looking for a new way to protect cigarettes from moisture and to replace the tin-lead wrappers in use at that time. In the 1920s, the price of aluminum dropped, and it clearly became the answer he was looking for. In addition to the price, aluminum was shinier and more appealing to consumers. Two decades later, Reynolds's company Reynolds Metals introduced the world to the lightweight, noncorrosive foil, Reynolds Wrap—and where would we be without it?

There is no proper side to a sheet of aluminum foil: The shiny side and the dull side function identically. One side comes in contact with a metallic roller during the manufacturing, and it becomes the shiny side; the duller side stays in contact with the conveyor belt. The shiny side being better for cooking food is just an old wives' tale.

How Much Was the Bill of Rights—and Who Paid It?

Some people argue that protecting freedoms of "religion, speech, assembly, press, and petition" were the most important issues, and that's why they're in the First Amendment. James Madison, who is credited with writing the Bill of Rights, initially proposed twelve amendments to the Constitution, but only ten were approved. The now-famous First Amendment was actually the Third Amendment in Madison's original draft. What were the first two? They dealt with congressional pay raises and reapportionment. So even at the beginning stages of our country, politicians were first and foremost interested in money and power.

Poison ivy isn't an ivy, and poison oak isn't an oak.
They are both anacardiaceous shrubs,
members of the cashew family.

The Number You Are Trying to Reach Is No Longer in Service

Alexander Graham Bell, who is credited with creating the telephone—or stealing the idea from Antonio Meucci, depending on how one looks at it—decided to cash out on the invention early by selling it to Western Union. One would think an invention of this importance would have been snatched up immediately—but surprisingly, Western Union just gave Bell static. The committee that was formed to review Bell's proposal stated the following:

> The telephone is named by its inventor A. G. Bell. He believes
> that one day they will be installed in every residence and place
> of business. . . . Bell's proposal to place his instrument in almost
> every home and business is fantastic. The central exchange alone
> would represent a huge outlay in real estate and buildings, to say
> nothing of the electrical equipment. In conclusion the committee
> feels that it must advise against any investment in Bell's scheme.
> We do not doubt that it will find users in special circumstances,
> but any development of the kind and scale which Bell so fondly
> imagines is utterly out of the question.

The people at Western Union must have been off their cradle.

Shaking Things Up

It's so common today that it's even referred to as common: common table salt. Salt is in such abundance these days, it only makes sense that it was always readily available—but it wasn't. In fact, salt was very expensive and not always easy to come by right up to the 1900s. Traders in ancient Greece bartered their slaves for salt; and a lazy or unruly slave was considered "not worth his salt"—an insult still in use today. Our word *salary* dates back to Roman times, when soldiers were paid an allowance, called, in Latin, a *salarium argentums* (which translates to "salt money"), so they could buy salt. The Latin words *salus,* for "well-being," and *salubritas,* for "health," both derive from the Latin *sal,* meaning "salt." In Mali, West Africa, salt was once worth its weight in gold; or another way of looking at it is that gold was worth its weight in salt.

Goldilocks was originally named Silver Hair.

Citizen Cane

 In the 1700s, a British gentleman had to buy a license for the privilege of carrying a walking stick and had to abide by a series of strict rules. In order to get the license, he had to agree not to gesture with or wave the walking stick in the air, hang it from his clothing, or tuck it under his arm. Very few gentlemen disregarded these rules, and there was never a cane mutiny.

In ancient times, it was believed that seeing your image on a shiny surface like a mirror or a calm pond of water would enable you to see the reflection of your spiritual self. It only made sense that if that were true, anything to disturb the image would bring bad luck to the physical body— this is where the superstition of seven years of bad luck from breaking a mirror originated.

Don't Be Such a Chicken

In the 1300s, the Black Death was treated with live pullets. The bird's tail feathers were plucked, and the bird was placed on the patient's infected sores. When the bird became infected and died, it was replaced with another. The "live pullet treatment" was believed to draw the poisons out of the patient—but it didn't work. The only plus side to this treatment was that it was more enjoyable to spend time with someone who had the plague if they had a chicken on their head.

Myth

If you touch a baby bird, its mother won't recognize
its scent and will abandon it.

Truth

No. Animals with a keen sense of smell, like dogs, might react negatively to the smell of another animal on their pups (they wouldn't abandon them, though), but birds have some of the poorest olfactory senses in the animal kingdom. Basically, you could rub dog poop on a chick, and its mom wouldn't know the foul smell from the fowl smell.

Here I Come to Save the Day!

The American Family Association (AFA), a watchdog group from Tupelo, Mississippi, filed a complaint with CBS about an episode of *Mighty Mouse: The New Adventure* cartoon that aired on April 23, 1988. The AFA complaint stated that the heroic rodent was seen snorting cocaine. The Reverend Donald Wildmon, on behalf of the AFA, described the questionable scene as follows: "Mighty Mouse is down in the dumps, and he reaches in his cape, pulls out a substance, and sniffs it through his nostrils, and from that point on in the cartoon he is his normal self." CBS producer Ralph Bakshi explained that in "The Little Tramp," Mighty Mouse was sad because he was in love with Polly Pineblossom but she didn't feel the same way about him. Polly had sold Mighty Mouse a broken and withered flower that turned to dust when he took it from her, and later on in the episode, he inhaled the flower pieces. The case never went to court, and Mighty Mouse was never called to the stand. One thing Reverend Wildmon never asked was what type of flower was it—I bet it was an opium poppy because everyone knows mice are hopheads.

Quotable Misquotes

Many actors are attributed with sayings, clever puns, or sharp-witted comebacks that they never actually said.
Like these:

- "Smile when you say that, pardner." What Gary Cooper really said to Walter Huston in the 1929 movie *The Virginian* was, "If you want to call me that, smile."
- "Me Tarzan, you Jane." In his first Tarzan role, Johnny Weissmuller's character wasn't even this articulate. In the 1932 film *Tarzan the Ape Man,* Weissmuller introduces himself to costar Maureen O'Sullivan by slapping his chest and saying, "Tarzan." He then gently pokes her on the chest and announces, "Jane."

Michelangelo is credited with having created the only shopping list known to have become a work of art. Michelangelo's cook was unable to read, so the Renaissance master drew a picture of wine, fruit, bread, and spaghetti— and you can bet it didn't land on someone's refrigerator door.

Quicker Than a Grindstone

At the beginning of the Victorian era in Great Britain, Thomas Saverland approached Caroline Newton in a jocular fashion and attempted to kiss her. She rejected his advances and then chewed him out—well, actually she just chewed off a piece of his nose. Saverland took Newton, the nose gnasher, to court in 1837, but she was acquitted. The judge ruled: "When a man kisses a woman against her will, she is fully entitled to bite his nose, if she so pleases." I wonder if the judge polled the jury and then counted the "ayes" and the "nose."

Chinese checkers did not originate in China, and the game doesn't use checkers. The game was created in England, and it is played with marbles on a star-shaped board. It was popular in the United States and even Japan long before the Chinese ever heard of it.

Daisy, Daisy, Give Me Your Answer Do

2001: A Space Odyssey is a 1968 science fiction film written by Arthur C. Clarke and Stanley Kubrick. In one scene, the HAL 9000, the talking supercomputer, contacts NASA to explain a malfunction with the sentence "Houston, we've got a problem." On April 13, 1970, while the crew of the ill-fated *Apollo 13* played "Thus Spake Zarathustra," the theme music from *2001: A Space Odyssey,* an oxygen tank in the service module exploded. Commander Jim Lovell contacted Mission Control to explain a malfunction with the sentence "Houston, we've had a problem."

If you suffer from triskaidekaphobia, a morbid fear of the number 13, you would have guessed that the space flight was in for trouble: *Apollo 13* launched at 13:13 Houston time, and the explosion occurred on April 13.

The Retriever of Zenda

In Pike County, Pennsylvania, in the summer of 1924, a neighbor of Governor and Mrs. Gifford Pinchot was accused of killing Mrs. Pinchot's cat. The governor was enraged and immediately had the crazed cat killer arrested, personally presiding over the murderer's hearing and then holding the case over for trial. The accused was allowed no legal counsel, and serving as judge and jury, Pinchot sentenced him to life imprisonment—the governor reportedly treated the defendant like a dog. Which in this case was fitting, because the accused was a dog, a male Labrador retriever named Pep. The dog was collared and taken to the state penitentiary in Philadelphia, where the warden, after being hounded by the governor to incarcerate the animal, finally gave Pep a prison ID, No. C2559. Since Pep was a male dog, he never became anybody's bitch—and after serving six years of his sentence in prison, Pep died of old age in 1930.

Myth

According to the Bible, angels have wings.

Truth

No. The Bible mentions angels but never describes them as having wings. This angelic image became popular because painters and sculptors took it upon themselves to give angels wings.

A Unique Groundbreaking Experiment

In 1958, a Boeing B-47E Stratojet accidentally released a nuclear bomb that landed in a Mars Bluff, South Carolina, family's vegetable garden—creating a thirty-five-foot-deep crater. The bomb exploded, destroying the house of Walter Greg and several other homes and injuring six people. Fortunately, the explosion was only the detonating device, which is TNT, and didn't trigger the nuclear material. Needless to say, Mr. Greg's tomatoes were ruined. Air force officials apologized.

❦

According to the Brookings Institution,
a Washington, D.C., think tank, the United States
lost eleven nuclear bombs in accidents during
the Cold War that were never recovered.

Knocking Over a Stonewall

During the Battle of Chancellorsville, on the night of May 2, 1863, Confederate General Thomas "Stonewall" Jackson took a small group of men to uncover a possible weakness in the Union's position. When he returned, he wasn't greeted by a hail of cheers but by a hail of bullets from a North Carolina regiment that thought he and his men were Yankee cavalrymen. Although his wounds didn't seem life threatening at first, Jackson contracted pneumonia after having his left arm amputated and died eight days later. So remind me what's so "friendly" about friendly fire.

"Government figures showed yesterday
that wholesale charges last month were at their
lowest level since the early seventies."
(*Daily Express*, 1/13/1987)

"The deceleration in wholesale price rises
is nearing its end."
(*Guardian*, 1/13/1987)

Stupid History

The Pride of Idaho

When a new territory in the Pike's Peak mining area, with Denver as its center, needed a name, Dr. George M. Willing, an eccentric lobbyist, suggested the name Idaho. Willing claimed the name was an Indian word meaning "Gem of the Mountains." But shortly before Congress agreed on the name, it was discovered that Dr. Willing had invented the word *Idaho*, and the territory became Colorado instead. However, two years later, when another mining territory in the Pacific Northwest needed a name, some remembered Idaho but forgot that the name had been a hoax—so on March 4, 1863, the territory of Idaho was established. When statehood was achieved in 1890, the name had stuck, and therefore the United States has a state based on a phony Indian name—possibly making it the greatest practical joke of all time.

The Douglas fir isn't a fir tree—it's actually a pine tree.

Indians with No Reservations

Naming Idaho might have been the greatest practical joke of all time—unless you look at the etymology of the name *Des Moines*. In June 1673, Father Jacques Marquette gathered with representatives of the Peoria Indian tribe near the mouth of what is now the Des Moines River. He asked the Peoria the name of their rival tribe that lived farther along the riverbank and was told they were called the Moingoana. (*Moines* was derived from this word.) But 330 years later, researcher Michael McCafferty of Indiana University, while researching the now-extinct Miami-Illinois language, and basing his conclusions on another linguist, David Costa, discovered that the literal translation of the word *Moingoana* is, in polite terms, "the excrement-faces."

Fortune cookies, along with the check, are the traditional conclusion to a Chinese dinner—or should I say the traditional American conclusion to a Chinese dinner. Fortune cookies were invented in the United States and are not served in China.

The Reflecting Pool

A party was thrown on August 1, 1985, for lifeguards of the New Orleans Recreation Department to celebrate their first season in which no one became a victim of drowning. Of the 200 partygoers, more than half were lifeguards, and four additional lifeguards were stationed on duty. When the party concluded, they were one guest less— thirty-one-year-old Jerome Moody was found dead on the bottom of the Recreation Department pool. File this one in the drawer marked *Irony.*

The Eighteenth Amendment to the Constitution (along with the Volstead Act, which defined "intoxicating liquors") was ratified on January 16, 1919. But not everyone wanted to jump off the wagon. Rhode Island never ratified the Eighteenth Amendment nor accepted the conditions of prohibition.

A Shot at Legal History

Clement L. Vallandigham (1820–1871) was a highly controversial Ohio politician who provoked much hostility by being a leader of the Copperhead faction of antiwar, pro-Confederate democrats during the American Civil War. Convicted as a traitor, his sentence of two years in prison was changed by President Abraham Lincoln to exile to the Confederacy. After the war, he moved back to Ohio and became a prominent lawyer who was known for his impassioned speeches, but during his final case, he really shot off his mouth. On the night before the trial, he was showing his colleagues that his client, Thomas McGehan, was innocent of murder and that the victim, Tom Myers, had actually shot himself. To demonstrate his theory, he shoved a pistol in his pocket, withdrew it, cocked the hammer, pronounced, "There, that's the way Myers held it," and pulled the trigger. The bullet entered Vallandigham's body just the way it entered Myers's, and the result was just as deadly. "My God, I've shot myself!" Vallandigham exclaimed. Shortly after this occurrence, and based on Vallandigham's deadly demonstration, his client, Thomas McGehan, was acquitted of all charges and released from custody. The judge rested the case, and Vallandigham rested in peace.

A Highly Charged Article

Alfred Nobel became a millionaire several times over and changed the face of mining, construction, and warfare as the inventor of dynamite. On April 12, 1888, Alfred's brother Ludwig died of heart trouble, and a leading French newspaper inadvertently ran an obituary on Alfred Nobel. "The merchant of death is dead," the article read. "Dr. Alfred Nobel, who became rich by finding ways to kill more people faster than ever before, died yesterday." Nobel was upset to find out not that he had died, but that, when his time was up, he would be remembered only as one who profited from death and destruction. To make sure that he was remembered fondly, Nobel bequeathed the bulk of his estate ($4,223,500—and remember that's 1896 money) to establish the Nobel prizes, awarded to those influential in advancing the causes of peace, literature, and the sciences. So in essence, Nobel had to die before he realized what his life was really about.

Starved for Attention

Sarah Jacobs, a Welsh teenager, became a celebrity in the 1870s for being able to go without eating for months at a time. Her parents put the young girl on exhibit, charged admission, and claimed their daughter had gone more than two years without eating a single piece of food. Spectators were intrigued by the emaciated girl, but Welsh officials were concerned the exhibit was a fraud and the young girl was in danger of starvation at the hands of her greedy parents. They placed Sarah under the care of a professional nurse, whose job it was to verify whether Sarah consumed anything—thereby proving one way or another if her parents were telling the truth. After nine days, officials were certain that Sarah's parents had been lying, and they were arrested and sent to prison for fraud. How did they know the claims were false? Because at the end of the ninth day, Sarah, who wasn't given any food during the observation, died of starvation. That'll show her parents!

Man Cannot Live by Bread Alone

In 1997, in suburban Bucks County, Pennsylvania, an alarming number of assaults were reported in supermarkets, grocery stores, and bakeries. The assaults weren't on women—they were on baked goods. Thanks to security cameras, the identity of the "Cookie Crumbler" was finally unwrapped—it was thirty-seven-year-old advertising executive Samuel Feldman. Feldman never squeezed the Charmin, but he did squeeze $800 worth of cookies, 3,087 loaves of bread, 227 bags of dinner rolls, 175 bags of bagels, and more, for a total of $7,000 worth of baked items. Feldman didn't gently caress the croissants or pet the pumpernickel, he squished everything so hard, it wasn't fit to sell and had to be discarded. At his trial in 2000, Sharon Feldman, Samuel's wife, came to his defense by pleading, "Freshness is important [to Samuel]." She tried to convince the jury her bread-abusing husband was only concerned his family had the freshest baked goods available. Sharon really buttered up the jury, and they almost rolled over in Samuel's favor, but the judge wasn't going to let this "loafer" off. He ruled that Feldman was guilty and his behavior was "not just odd, it was criminal." I wonder if he was sentenced to just bread and water.

Or Is It a Repocracy?

If the United States is a democracy, then the Founding Fathers must have believed a democratic country was the way to go, right? First of all, the United States of America isn't a democracy—it's a republic. (Remember, "and to the republic for which it stands.") The men who framed the Constitution disagreed on a lot of things, but on one point they stood united—that a democracy was the worst possible form of government. The idea that our country is built on "majority rules" is far from the truth. The Founding Fathers knew that a democracy would quickly lead to mob rule—that's why our system of government is set up the way it is. We elect senators and congresspeople to represent us in Washington, D.C.; we vote for them, and they're supposed to vote the way we want. If they don't vote the way we want, we vote them out of office at the next election. It's that simple and that complicated—but it's still not a democracy.

Can't Keep a Good Man Down

Did you ever wonder where Edgar Allan Poe got his inspiration when writing ghoulish tales of people buried alive like "The Premature Burial"? Well, it wasn't all fiction in the days before modern medicine and proper embalming techniques. In fact, several ingenious inventors patented, for the nearly departed, "grave signals"—or what I like to call "Dead Ringers." The first such patent, from 1843, was a spring-loaded coffin lid (good only before one is buried, of course). In 1868, Newark, New Jersey, inventor Franz Vester patented a postburial contraption that consisted of a tube directly over the face that

> extends from the coffin up through and over the surface of the
> grave, said tube containing a ladder and cord, one end of said
> cord being placed in the hand of the person laid in the coffin
> and the other end of said cord being attached to a bell on top of
> the square tube, so that, should a person be interred ere life is
> extinct, he can, on recovery to consciousness, ascend from the
> grave by the ladder; or, if not able to ascend by said ladder, ring
> the bell, thereby giving an alarm and thus saving himself.

And just in case you're wondering, "saved by the bell" did not originate from these grave signals—it originated from the ringing of the bell during a boxing match.

More Quotable Misquotes

"Why don't you come up and see me sometime?" The public must not have liked the sentence structure of Mae West's seductive invitation to Cary Grant in the 1933 movie *She Done Him Wrong*. Ever since she first uttered the line, it was misquoted—what she really said was, "Why don't you come up sometime and see me?"

And speaking of Cary Grant, he never spoke the phrase "Judy, Judy, Judy" that imitators (and Goober from *The Andy Griffith Show*) always use to portray him.

English muffins are popular in the United States but not popular in England. Why? Because the English didn't invent the English muffin—if they had, they would have just called it a muffin. The closest thing in England would be a crumpet—not an English crumpet . . . just a crumpet.

In Case of Emergency, Break Glass

The award for weirdest "deceased detector" goes to a device patented in 1899 by M. C. H. Nicolle of France. His creation utilized a hammer that, activated by any movement of the corpse, would swing down and break a glass window situated over the head of the departed. This would allow air to enter the coffin, and the noise of the breaking glass would serve as an alarm (used only before burial). I have a grave concern about this invention: If anyone did awaken from a coma and try to sit up, his or her head would smash through the glass window, followed shortly by a solid clobbering by the hammer. But what better place to be for such an occurrence than in a coffin and already dressed up?

Nothing up My Sleeve, Nothing in My Head

In 1977, a woman calling herself a "psychic escapologist" announced she was going to drive a car sixty miles per hour over a course of one mile while wearing a blindfold. Her only source of direction, she boasted, was by tapping into the minds of people in the crowd, who would communicate to her which way to turn. "No sooner had I started than I felt myself reading the mind of someone in the crowd," the psychic steerer said. "This thought-transferee began by giving me explicit instructions. But just as the alarm bell told me I had reached fifty, they stopped beaming." Although her GPS (Group Paranormal Supervision) was out of whack, she felt compelled to corner the car—which she did, right into the corner of a barn. The psychic was knocked unconscious and was taken to a hospital to recover from her extensive injuries. She assured her fans she would soon complete the rest of her planned routine—escaping from a large, heavy-duty plastic bag in only twenty minutes. The one thing this psychic escapologist couldn't escape was her own stupidity.

Digging for Research

Of all the topics for a scientific study, why did researchers at the University of Wisconsin–Madison pick rhinotillexomania? The answer was right in front of their noses—*rhinotillexomania* is the scientific term for what we laypeople call "nose picking" (or "snotis-diggus-outis"). In 1990, the university mailed out questionnaires to 1,200 people trying to dig up the answers to such penetrating questions as "What finger do you use when picking your nose?" and "After picking your nose, how often do you find yourself looking at what you have removed?" And of course the question on everybody's mind: "Did you eat it?"

❧❦☙

January 4, 1961, was a great day for all the longhairs in Copenhagen, Denmark—it was the day that barbers' assistants ended their thirty-three-year-long strike.

A Very Queer Relationship.

The truth may never come out of the closet on this one, but then again there might not have been a closet to come out of. It's the story of two men: James Buchanan and William Rufus de Vane King. One became the fifteenth president of the United States; the other, vice president under Franklin Pierce. But when they first met each other while serving as members of Congress, they became immediately inseparable. It has been rumored for years that Buchanan and King were a "couple," but it's never been proven—Buchanan was, however, the only bachelor ever elected president. What is known is that Buchanan and King were commonly referred to by other members of Congress as "Mr. Buchanan and his wife" and "Miss Nancy and Aunt Fancy." So when Buchanan was passing legislation in Congress and King said, "I've got your back," he might have meant something completely different.

East Is East and West Is West

In studying the history of America's western expansion, you'll inevitably hear or read Horace Greeley's immortal line "Go west, young man." And as you've probably guessed by now, Mr. Greeley never said this particular line—he did, however, write it. You see, John Babsone Soule first wrote this advice in an article in Indiana's *Terre Haute Express* in 1851, and Horace Greeley reprinted the article in his *New York Tribune*. In Greeley's reprint, he pointed out that Soule was the original author of the article and the quote—but that didn't stop the general public from giving Greeley all the credit, and now the quote and the man who reprinted it are forever synonymous.

In 1205, Moloji Thorat filed a lawsuit in India and was amazed at how slowly the wheels of the legal system turned. So slowly did they turn that it took 751 years for them to come full circle and reach a judgment on the case. The courts ruled in Thorat's favor and in 1966 paid an undisclosed sum of rupees to his family.

He Was Still a Brave Soul

Sitting Bull, Pocahontas, Tecumseh, Iron Eyes Cody—these are some of the more famous Indians (American Indians or Native Americans, to you PCers) that leap to most people's minds when questioned. Iron Eyes Cody, if you don't remember, acted in nearly 100 movies but was probably most famous as the "crying Indian" of the Keep America Beautiful ad campaign "People Start Pollution, People Can Stop It" that first aired in 1971. But there's one thing about Iron Eyes that sets him apart from other famous American Indians—he wasn't an American Indian. Iron Eyes was born Espera "Oscar" DeCorti in Kaplan, Louisiana, in 1904 to Italian immigrant parents (father, Antonio DeCorti, and mother, Francesca Salpietra). Iron Eyes assumed his Indian identity in the 1920s in order to get acting work in Hollywood films. From then until he was laid to rest in 1999, Iron Eyes insisted he was a member of the Cherokee tribe—and everyone believed him. In fact, in 1995, Hollywood's American Indian community honored Iron Eyes for his long-standing contribution to American Indian causes. The question isn't "why" Iron Eyes posed as an Indian all those years, the real question is "how."

So What's Your Act Called? The Aristocats!

The Life and Adventures of a Cat was a "racy" and risqué book published in England in 1760. The book centered on a ram cat (the name male cats went by back then) named Tom the Cat. The book was so amazingly popular that from that point on, male cats have been commonly called *tomcats*.

Maryland is the only state in the contiguous United States with an official state sport. The sport of Maryland? Jousting. Yes, guys on horses with long pointy sticks charging each other. I suppose Maryland is also the gateway to Dork City.

Old Flames Burn the Brightest

All our lives, we've heard about the Seven Wonders of the Ancient World: the Great Pyramid of Giza, the Hanging Gardens of Babylon, the Statue of Zeus at Olympia, the Temple of Artemis at Ephesus, the Mausoleum at Halicarnassus, the Colossus of Rhodes, and the Lighthouse of Alexandria. Of these seven wonders, only one is still standing—the Great Pyramid of Giza. (All the others were destroyed by fire or earthquake.) The Temple of Artemis at Ephesus burned to the ground in 356 B.C. when an arsonist, hoping his name would live forever for his destructive feat, put a torch to it. The arsonist was executed, and to make sure his wish of everlasting fame wouldn't come true, it was ordered that his name be stricken from all records and never mentioned again. But you know how people talk. Despite all their best efforts, the man's name leaked out, and Herostratus, the arsonist, is remembered as one of the most notorious firebugs in history.

Wrong Place at the Wrong Time— Three Times Running

Robert Todd Lincoln, Abraham Lincoln's eldest son, is the only person to have been at the scene of three presidential assassinations. On April 14, 1865, the day his father was shot, Robert Todd rushed to Ford's Theatre to be with his fatally injured father. In 1881, he was in the room with President James Garfield the day Garfield was assassinated. And twenty years later, he was to join President William McKinley at the Pan American Exposition, arriving shortly after McKinley was assassinated. There are many a mysterious and bizarre happenstance about Abraham Lincoln's life and death, and so too with Robert Todd. You see, the son of the president would never have witnessed any of these assassinations had he not narrowly escaped death at a young age. While standing on a crowded railroad platform, he stumbled and nearly fell onto the tracks. He was grabbed by the back of the shirt and pulled to safety in the nick of time. The person who saved his life was Edwin Booth—the brother of John Wilkes Booth. Yeah, I got chill bumps, too!

No, I'm Talking About the Kind That Holds Back Water

Near the Spaarndam lock, in the municipality of Haarlem in the Netherlands, stands a statue of Hans Brinker, undoubtedly the most famous boy in Dutch history. You might not know his name, but if I said, "He stuck his finger in a dike," you'd know to whom I'm referring. American author Mary Mapes Dodge first published *Hans Brinker, or the Silver Skates* in 1865, and it soon became a favorite of American schoolchildren. After that, when Americans visited Haarlem, they asked the locals to direct them to the location where the courageous boy heroically saved their town. Instead of getting directions, visiting Americans usually got blank stares. Why? Because there was never a Hans Brinker. But after years of trying to convince foreigners that the story was made up, not part of Dutch history, and written by an American, they finally gave up—and put up a statue in 1950. I never fingered Hans Brinker as a hero as much as a blockhead—if he had been really smart, he would have stuck a rock in the hole and gone to get help.

A Grain of Truth

What does "sow wild oats" mean? Okay, we know the phrase means to commit youthfully foolish acts, but what does that have to do with sowing (not sewing) wild oats? During the eleventh century, many farmers and peasants left their farms to fight against a multitude of armies who were perpetually invading England. With the farms unattended, many of the domesticated grains reverted to their wild strains. When the warring settled down, a lot of the younger men were eager to settle down, and with no experience in farming, they began collecting and planting the seeds from the wild strains of oats. The plants produced were basically useless, as they grew very few "heads" that contained the edible seeds. So it was foolish of these inexperienced young men to waste their time sowing wild oats.

Presidential Poundage

Someone's got to have the distinction of being the fattest president, and that honor goes to William Howard Taft. Taft varied in weight from 300 to more than 350 pounds (when he was depressed). One day, President Taft relaxed in the presidential bathtub to soak off the stress of the day—and stayed there for longer than he had anticipated. He was stuck. It was an embarrassing thing to have happen, and as soon as he was rescued, he ordered an enormous, personalized tub for himself. The J. L. Mott ironworks made the tub to Taft's specifications and installed it in the White House. When it was being delivered, four White House staffers had their photograph taken—all four men fit comfortably inside the new tub. This is possibly where the nickname "Tubby" came from.

Springtime for Hitler

In most film studies of World War II, one will inevitably see the infamous footage of Adolf Hitler doing a bizarre little victory jig after the French government surrendered to Germany on June 22, 1940. What's interesting about the Footloose Führer (or the Two-Stepping Goose-Stepper) is that the film was actually a little propaganda fakery. Hitler forced the French government to surrender in the same railroad car in Compiègne, France, where Germany had signed the armistice in 1918 that ended World War I. When he emerged from the railroad car, Hitler leaped slightly, and that's all the Allied film propagandists needed. They took the single jump and looped the film over and over to give the illusion that Hitler was dancing (like the dancing cats on the Purina Cat Chow commercials). The film had the desired effect. Hitler's silly dance proved to everyone how monstrously childish Hitler really was and solidified in the minds of Americans, who hadn't entered the war, that he was a deranged sissy-man.

Dogs of War

Pop quiz: What started the War of the Stray Dog? What? Never heard of the War of the Stray Dog? On October 22, 1925, a Greek soldier ran after his dog across the border separating Macedonia from Petrich in Bulgaria. A Bulgarian sentry shot the Greek soldier (no word on what happened to the dog), which prompted Greece to declare war and invade Bulgaria. They quickly occupied Petrich but left the area a week later under the pressure of the League of Nations. The League sanctioned Greece, demanding both immediate withdrawal and compensation to Bulgaria. Greece agreed to the terms and paid Bulgaria £45,000. The War of the Stray Dog, also known as the Incident at Petrich, claimed the lives of fifty people before Greece withdrew its forces.

I Only Get It for the Articles Anyway

On the cover of every *Saturday Evening Post* from 1899 to its demise was the claim: "Founded A.D. 1728 by Benjamin Franklin." This would have come as a shock to Franklin, as he never heard of the *Saturday Evening Post* due to the fact that he had died in 1790, thirty-one years before its first issue—on August 4, 1821. The only possible connection between the *Saturday Evening Post* and Benjamin Franklin is that in 1729 (not 1728), Franklin took over a struggling newspaper, the *Pennsylvania Gazette,* which continued publication until 1800—and the *Post* used the same print shop that the *Gazette* formerly used. This is a case of either six degrees of separation or 200 years of lying.

A Voyage of Titanic Proportions

It's either a case of the worst luck in history or the best:

- In 1829, a ship called *The Mermaid* was four days away from her destination of Sydney, Australia, when a massive storm struck and drove the ship into a reef. All twenty-two people on board survived and were able to swim to safety.
- Three days later, the *Swiftsure* rescued them.
- Five days later, the *Swiftsure* sank.
- Victims from both ships were rescued by the schooner *Governor Ready.*
- Three hours later, the *Governor Ready* caught fire.
- The *Comet* pulled everyone from lifeboats and brought them aboard.
- Five days later, the *Comet* sank. (The crew went for help in the longboat, leaving the passengers floating in the water.)
- Eighteen hours later, the mail boat *Jupiter* pulled everyone out of the ocean.
- In under twelve hours, the *Jupiter* sank.
- Everyone was rescued by the passenger vessel *The City of Leeds.*
- Four days later, *The City of Leeds* docked in Sydney, Australia.

The bad luck was that five ships were lost—the good luck was that not a single person died.

He Was a Dick
from the Very Start

"Wanted: Congressional candidate with no previous political experience to defeat a man who has represented the district in the House for 10 years," read an ad that appeared in several southern California newspapers in 1946. "Any young man, resident of district, preferably a veteran, fair education, may apply for the job." The ad wasn't a joke. The Republican Party, in hopes of finding a maverick politician to defeat incumbent Congressman Jerry Voorhis, had placed it. To everyone's surprise, a maverick politician did answer the ad—and did go on to defeat Voorhis for California's Twelfth Congressional District. The want-ad-answering politician's name . . . Richard M. Nixon.

No Return—No Deposit

In January 1995, Mill Valley, California, court commissioner Randolph Heubach ruled that a landlord had the legal right to keep the $825 security deposit because the former tenant left without giving thirty-days' notice. It sounds like a no-brainer until you find out the reason the man didn't give notice—he had died. After tenant James Pflugradt succumbed to a heart attack, his son, Rick, cleaned out the apartment and asked the landlord for his father's security deposit back. The landlord, Fred Padula, refused on the grounds that he wasn't given proper notice and needed the money to cover rent while he found a new tenant. "I am not unsympathetic," said Heubach after his ruling. "But it is really a straightforward financial situation." Rick Pflugradt, who was out $825 and a father on the deal, stated, "This sends my faith in the human race to an all-time low." I hate to say this, but what did Pflugradt expect—he was dealing with a lawyer and a landlord.

Not the Boys in the Hood—
But the Boys Under the Hood

After a lengthy court battle, the Missouri Ku Klux Klan was granted permission, in March 2000, to participate in the state's Adopt-a-Highway program. This victory would force the state to use taxpayer money to place Adopt-a-Highway road signs on a one-mile stretch of road advertising the KKK. The Klan's victory was crossed out the following month when their organization was removed from the program. The reason? The state legislature decided to name the Klan's designated portion of road (I-55 south of St. Louis) after civil rights activist Rosa Parks—and the Klan never showed up to clean. I suppose the only cleansing the Klan is interested in is racial cleansing.

You Say Tomato and I Say . . . Tomato

It's a battle that's been fought for ages—is a tomato a vegetable or a fruit? To the smart aleck who says a tomato is a fruit because it grows on a vine, I say, you're wrong . . . and you're right. A tomato, according to botanists, *is* a fruit not because it grows on a vine but because it is considered the "ovary" of the plant (the part containing the seeds). So next time Mr. Know-It-All says a tomato is a fruit, you can tell him so are pumpkins, cucumbers, peas, and corn. A vegetable, in case you're wondering, is any other part of the plant that is edible: the leaves, the stems, and the roots.

When the Chips Are Down

On June 3, 1980, computers alerted the U.S. Strategic Air Command (SAC) in Omaha, Nebraska, that a Soviet submarine missile attack was in progress. One hundred B-52s were scrambled and in the air within a matter of minutes, but were called off before they could launch a counterattack. Which was a good thing, because there was no Soviet missile attack, and it wasn't a war game, either—it was a faulty computer chip. A 46¢ computer chip had malfunctioned and caused the computer to nearly start World War III. Everyone at SAC breathed a sigh of relief until three days later, when the same mistake happened again.

How Do You Know He's a King? He Hasn't Got Sh*t All Over Him

Life must have been simpler in the good ol' days: They didn't have computers and Blackberrys and traffic and the normal frantic hustle and bustle of modern times. Of course, we don't get crap thrown on us, so that pretty much makes up the difference in my mind. It was a centuries-long practice throughout Europe, although officially banned in 1395 in Paris, to open your window or door and toss out the contents of your chamber pot into the street. Let me give you a minute to let that sink in. Of course, proper etiquette was to yell "Gardez l'eau!" (watch out for the water) to give passersby time to duck and cover. And if people were like they are today, I'll bet not everyone gave a warning before they flung poo.

The Department of Redundancy Department

To project "a greater openness and sense of public responsibility," the CIA commissioned a task force to study ways to help them change their cloak-and-dagger persona. On December 20, 1991, the committee presented its findings in the fifteen-page "Task Force Report on Greater Openness." The CIA took the document, classified and stamped it *SECRET,* and has refused to divulge or comment on its contents.

Live from the Pasta Farms, This Has Been Al Dente

The British Broadcasting Corporation (BBC) aired a documentary on its news show *Panorama* about spaghetti growers in Switzerland—on April 1, 1957. The joke broadcast showed Swiss spaghetti farmers picking fresh spaghetti from "spaghetti trees" and preparing the spaghetti for market. It also mentioned that the pasta farmers had a bumper crop partly because of the "virtual disappearance of the spaghetti weevil." Soon after the broadcast, the BBC received phone calls from viewers eager to know if spaghetti really grew on trees and how they might go about growing a spaghetti tree of their own. To this last question, the BBC reportedly replied that they should "place a sprig of spaghetti in a tin of tomato sauce and hope for the best."

It's Not Just a Good Book—
It's a Great Book!

In 1631, King Charles I ordered 1,000 Bibles from an English printer named Robert Barker. Printing was not an exact science in those days, and sometimes mistakes were made and usually overlooked—but not in this case. Barker inadvertently left out a single word in the Seventh Commandment in Exodus 20:14—the word *not*. Readers were shocked to find out that God had commanded Moses "Thou shalt commit adultery" as opposed to "Thou shalt not commit adultery." King Charles was not amused by this mistake and ordered all the Bibles destroyed, fined Barker 300 pounds sterling (a lifetime's wages in those days), and revoked his printing license—Barker was out of business. Not all the Bibles were destroyed; there are eleven known to still exist. Because of the infamous mistake, this printing of the official King James Version is referred to as "The Wicked Bible."

Because They Don't Know the Words

Tesco, an international supermarket chain based in the United Kingdom and Britain's largest retailer, published an advertisement in *The Sun* announcing their newest product—whistling carrots. The genetically modified carrot, the ad explained, was specially engineered to grow with airholes along its side that acted like little whistles. When placed in a pot to boil or in a steamer, the carrots whistled like a teakettle to let the cook know they were done. If this were true, it would be great—not as a self-cooking vegetable, but to use on a snowman to make it seem like he's got a clogged nose.

Better Than the Best

History books have idolized our founding fathers to such a degree that a lot of people believe they were perfect. Simply by looking at the first line of the Constitution you'll find that they weren't perfect—and they especially weren't more perfect. The first line of the preamble to the Constitution reads, "We the people of the United States, in order to form a more perfect union." If something is perfect it's, well, perfect—it can't be *more* perfect. Ask any English teacher, and they will tell you that "more perfect" ain't good English.

⁂

Andrew Jackson's wife, Rachel, was
the only first lady who smoked a pipe.

Better Late Than Never

General Andrew "Old Hickory" Jackson (he got his nickname because he was as hard as old hickory) was victorious over the invading British Army intent on seizing New Orleans during the War of 1812. The infamous Battle of New Orleans was an enormous boost, not necessarily to the war effort, but to the future career of Andrew Jackson. Jackson used his war hero status during his biggest battle ever—the battle to become the seventh president of the United States (1829–1837). But was the Battle of New Orleans even an important battle? Not really. The war was already over before the Battle of New Orleans began. The Treaty of Ghent, which officially ended the War of 1812, had been signed on December 24, 1814; the Battle of New Orleans took place on January 8, 1815.

Having the Last Word

What a man decides to have put on his tombstone says a lot about what was important in his life. One would think that a man like Thomas Jefferson might need several tombstones to cover all the accomplishments of which he was proud. Surprisingly, the inscription that Jefferson personally wrote left out a few key things. His tombstone reads: "Here was buried Thomas Jefferson, author of the Declaration of American Independence, of the Statute of Virginia for Religious Freedom, and Father of the University of Virginia." You'll notice that he doesn't mention that he was the second vice president of the United States or even that he was the third president.

A Town by Any Other Name

When the Pilgrims finally landed and settled in Plymouth, Massachusetts, in 1620 (after having originally been dumped in Provincetown, Massachusetts, because the crew of the *Mayflower* was tired of their complaining), they named the city Plymouth because they had set sail from Plymouth, England. It makes perfect sense and is widely believed, but it's not true. The city was already named Plymouth. In 1614, Captain John Smith mapped out the northeast coast of North America starting from Jamestown, Virginia, and he returned to England with a map on which most landmarks had, of course, Indian names. Smith asked Prince Charles to replace the "barbarous" Native American names with good old-fashioned English ones, and His Royal Highness obliged. When Prince Charles came to the Native American name "Accomack" on the map, he decided to change it to Plymouth. The fact that the *Mayflower* set sail from Plymouth, England, and landed in Plymouth, Massachusetts, is just a fun fluke in American history.

Doubleday Double Play

When asked, "Who invented baseball?" most people would answer, "Abner Doubleday," and most people would be wrong. Baseball was invented in England (gasp!). It was first named and described in 1744 in *A Little Pretty Pocket Book*, which was reprinted in the United States in 1762. So how did Abner Doubleday get credit for inventing a game that had been around for nearly a hundred years? It was a propaganda campaign. The Major League's executive board, wanting to score a home run by claiming baseball had been invented in America, commissioned a report on the game's origin in 1907. In this report, baseball was first credited with being the brainchild of Civil War general and hero Abner Doubleday in Cooperstown, New York, in 1839. Even though Doubleday never mentioned inventing baseball in his diaries, or the fact that he never visited Cooperstown. Makes you wonder about the origins of apple pie and Chevrolet now, doesn't it?

Bases Loaded

So who should get credit for inventing baseball? Most authorities now agree that Alexander Cartwright, a Manhattan bookseller, should get the credit for inventing the modern game of baseball. In 1842 he founded the Knickerbocker Baseball Club, named after the Knickerbocker Fire Engine Company, for which he was a volunteer. Cartwright drew the first diagram of the diamond-shaped field and the rules of the modern game are based on bylaws his team created. He was finally inducted into the Baseball Hall of Fame in 1938.

In 1989, George Herbert Walker Bush was the first vice president elected to the office of the presidency since Martin Van Buren in 1836.

Bedford Falls

The warm-hearted fantasy *It's a Wonderful Life*, produced and directed by Frank Capra for Liberty Films, was nominated for five Oscars (without winning any) and is recognized by the American Film Institute as one of the 100 best American films ever made. It is placed number one on their list of the most inspirational American films of all time. But when it was first released on December 20, 1946, it was considered a flop. The movie cost $2,300,000 and grossed only about $2,000,000 during its initial release—less than half of what Liberty Films expected.

~❀~

On June 28, 1836, James Madison's last words were "I always talk better lying down."

Losing His Marbles

In April 1841, Vice President John Tyler was on his knees playing marbles when he was informed that William Henry Harrison had died, and he was now president of the United States. At that time, marbles was a very popular game for both children and grown-ups.

Let Freedom Ring

On July 8, 1776, the grand peal of the Liberty Bell alerted citizens that the country they lived in was now independent, while the founding fathers read to them the Declaration of Independence that freed them from the tyranny of British rule. But the story just doesn't ring true. It's true that the bell was hanging in the Philadelphia statehouse at the time, but no one rang it. Why would they? It had a huge crack in it from a forging error and, at that time, was not a symbol of freedom or liberty. The name Liberty Bell wasn't adopted until 1839 in a pamphlet entitled *The Liberty Bell, by Friends of Freedom*, where it symbolized the liberty of black slaves, not the independence of white Americans from Britain. Until that time it was called the State House Bell—because it hung in the statehouse.

Stay Tuned

Television was first demonstrated to the general public at the 1939 New York World's Fair. But not everyone who tuned in was turned on. One critic from the *New York Times* remarked that television would never actually compete with radio because "people must sit and keep their eyes glued on a screen; the average American family hasn't the time for it."

Birds of a Feather

Confederate General Richard Ewell was an odd-looking fellow with a beak-like nose and a bald head that he would cock to one side when he was speaking. Because he had lost a leg in a previous battle, he hopped around camp like a parakeet. Ewell fought bravely at Gettysburg, but he had such a nervous disposition that he found it difficult to sleep in a normal position and would curl around a stool instead of lying in his cot. He had convinced himself that he had some mysterious internal "disease," and his diet consisted almost entirely of frumenty, hulled wheat boiled in milk and sweetened with sugar. It was also reported from camp guards that Ewell would sit in his tent for hours alone—quietly chirping to himself.

Apparently more Catholics attended Mass during Prohibition than any time in American history—because the production of legal sacramental wine increased by hundreds of thousands of gallons during that time.

Another Briquette in the Wall

What do you get when you combine the foremost American inventor and America's foremost car manufacturer? Would you believe the charcoal briquette? Thomas Edison and Henry Ford are credited with making, from sawdust and glue from Ford's factory floor and Edison's creative wizardry, the infamous barbecue fuel. They made it, but they got the idea from someone else: Ellsworth B. A. Zwoyer, who invented, designed, and patented the original briquette in 1897. The mystery as to why Ford and Edison decided to make their own charcoal briquettes has a simple solution— they took the idea from one of their friends, Ellsworth Zwoyer.

What Comes Around

As President John Adams and his wife, Abigail, traveled home from Philadelphia (then the capital) to Braintree, Massachusetts, they passed through Newark, New Jersey, and the town celebrated the occasion with pomp and ceremony. But not everyone enjoyed seeing the Federalist president, especially Republican Luther Baldwin, who stumbled out of John Burnet's dram shop and stared drunkenly at the commotion. Hearing the sixteen-gun salute and knowing Baldwin's hatred of the president, one customer exclaimed, "There goes the president and they are firing at his ass." To which Baldwin chimed, "I don't care if they fire through his ass!" With that remark, Baldwin was immediately arrested under the new Alien and Sedition laws (similar to the modern Patriot Act) for uttering "seditious words tending to defame the President and Government of the United States." Baldwin was fined, assessed court costs, and sent to a federal jail until he made financial amends.

Rumors of My Death Have Been Exaggerated

In 1800, newspapers across the United States printed the sad news that Vice President Thomas Jefferson had died at Monticello (his estate in Virginia) after a brief illness. From the moment the article was first printed in a Baltimore paper on June 30 and for an entire week some people were grief stricken, some were doubtful about the story, and some, mainly Jefferson's enemies, were hopeful. It turned out that Thomas Jefferson had died as reported, but it wasn't Thomas Jefferson the author of the Declaration of Independence—it was one of Thomas Jefferson's slaves who shared the same name. It was twenty-six years before Thomas Jefferson died in 1826—on July 4.

❧

George Herbert Walker Bush
is the only president with four names.

The Black and Red of It All

On January 8, 1835, the United States under President Andrew Jackson, for the first and only time, completely paid off its national debt (well, actually we still owed $33,733.05, but who's counting?). This was accomplished through the sale of public lands in the West. The country was debt free for only a short time, and then it rapidly went millions of dollars into the red.

On May 16, 1974, Richard Kleindienst, John Mitchell's successor as attorney general after the Watergate scandal, pled guilty to a misdemeanor charge of failing to accurately testify before a Senate committee. Kleindienst is the first attorney general ever convicted of a crime.

Don't Flip Your Whig

When the Whig party nominated Zachary Taylor as its presidential candidate in early June 1848, they sent him a letter notifying him of their choice, and he sent the letter back. Why? Because at that time, recipients of letters paid the postage, not the person sending the letter. In fact, the first stamp was issued only one year before Taylor's nomination, but the practice of recipient-paid postage still continued. Because Taylor was extremely popular as one of the heroes of the Mexican-American War (I guess you could say he was a Big Whig), he received a great deal of fan mail for which he would have had to pay the postage. So he routinely returned all the mail he received, including the nomination. It wasn't until July that Taylor learned he was the official candidate for the Whig Party. He went on to become president in 1849 and was the last Whig ever elected.

The Ride of Your Life

When most Americans think about a heroic horseback ride to warn citizens of a British invasion, they think of Paul Revere. But Revere only rode nineteen miles before he was captured. So why do we remember him, and not the truly heroic 345-mile ride by Israel Bissell? Who? Bissell, a twenty-three-year-old postal rider, rode four days and six hours (April 19, 1775–April 23, 1775) from Boston to Philadelphia, warning the citizens of each town he rode through by shouting, "To arms, to arms. The war has begun." He was so underappreciated for his bravery that in several historical documents his first name was inaccurately listed as Trail.

Until 1900, the state of Rhode Island had two capitals, one at Providence and the other at Newport.

Grant Your Wishes

Some people, mainly Republicans, charged John Kennedy with nepotism when he asked his brother Bobby to serve as attorney general. But the king of keeping it in the family was Republican President Ulysses S. Grant. Grant placed his father on the payroll as postmaster at Covington, Kentucky; his wife's brother-in-law James Casey was appointed collector of customs to the Port of New Orleans; another brother-in-law served as appraiser of customs in San Francisco; his cousin Silas Hudson was named a minister to Guatemala; and another brother-in-law was minister to Denmark. In all, nearly forty people associated with Grant, including thirteen relatives, benefited from "Grantism."

***

George Washington was the first and only president to
have been elected by a unanimous electoral vote.

A Chamber Musician

On January 23, 1978, Terry Kath, lead guitarist for the rock group Chicago, was playing around with a .38 revolver during a party. As a joke, he put the gun to his head and pulled the trigger. Kath, a gun enthusiast, then picked up a 9mm semi-automatic pistol and prepared to do the same thing but was asked by the party's host to stop. Kath deftly removed the gun's clip, reassured the host by saying, "Don't worry, it's not loaded," and proceeded to shoot himself in the head. Even though Kath had removed the magazine he had forgotten to unload the chamber and was killed instantly.

In 1908, the grandnephew of
Napoleon Bonaparte, Charles Joseph
Bonaparte, created the Bureau
of Investigation, which would later
become known as the FBI.

A Slave to the Past

When they were boys, future Presidents Millard Fillmore and Andrew Johnson were indentured servants. An indentured servant is a laborer under contract to an employer for a specified period of time, usually three to seven years, in exchange for necessities such as food, drink, clothing, transportation, and lodging. The master basically owned the indentured servant, who had hardly any rights, until the term of the contract was met. Andrew Johnson was indentured to a tailor, and he ran away. The tailor placed an advertisement in the *Raleigh Gazette* (North Carolina), offering a reward of $10 for the capture and return of the future President Johnson. Fillmore served his master, a cloth maker, for several years and was able to purchase his freedom for $30. Sometimes I wonder if we would have been better off if they had stayed indentured servants.

Out of the Mouth of Abe

It's a well-told story that President Abraham Lincoln once responded to complaints about the drinking habits of General Ulysses S. Grant by saying, "If I knew what brand he used, I'd send every other general in the field a barrel of it." It's a great story and really exemplifies Lincoln's sense of humor, but according to David Homer Bates's book *Lincoln Stories*, Lincoln's response when asked if he had ever made this infamous quip was that he never had said it. Well, at least he was honest.

A Graham of Goodness

Presbyterian minister Reverend Sylvester Graham developed the graham cracker in Bound Brook, New Jersey, in 1822, but it wasn't to complete the recipe for S'mores. In fact, it was created so that people wouldn't want s'more of anything—especially sex. Graham believed his cracker, along with bland foods and a strict vegetarian diet, could cure not only alcoholism but more important, sexual urges (which he believed to be the source of many maladies). Graham's belief that eating pure foods created a purity of mind, spirit, and body influenced several people, including Dr. John Harvey Kellogg, the inventor of the corn flakes breakfast cereal.

In 1871, Tucson, Arizona, was the heart of the Wild West, and boasted 3,000 people, two doctors, a newspaper, a brewery, and several salons— but just one bathtub.

A Vein Endeavor

Bloodletting, or bleeding, is now considered an antiquated, useless, and dangerous (sometimes deadly) form of medicine. A great deal of blood is drawn from the patient in the hope that it will balance the four humors of the body (black bile, yellow bile, phlegm, and blood) that were thought to control all bodily functions. Surprisingly, people still practiced bloodletting up into the twentieth century, as this ad from the 1905 Sears catalog proves: "Spring Bleeding Lance. The only practicable, safe and convenient instrument for bleeding on the market. Used almost exclusively by old school physicians for the purpose." Still, it sounds better than one of the other old school practices—leeches.

Don't Be Such a Baby!

It's true that Dr. Benjamin Spock was an American pediatrician whose book *Baby and Child Care*, published in 1946, is one of publishing's best sellers of all time. But what's not true is the rumor that he was jailed for his anti-Vietnam point of view during the 1960s. Spock was arrested in 1968 and convicted on charges of conspiring to advise young men to avoid the draft, but he appealed the verdict, and his conviction was reversed the following year.

Before Spock's groundbreaking childcare book was published, John B. Watson's 1928 book *Psychological Care of Infant and Child* was used widely in American hospitals and contained such stern advice as, "Never kiss your children."

Hi Hoe, Hi Hoe

On December 25, 1790, twenty-five girls from an asylum in Paris, France, called the Saltpêtrière were sent to the Louisiana colony in America because there were so few women. By their action, the French government also hoped to lure Canadian settlers away from Indian mistresses.

Selling Yourself Short

Henry John Heinz, president of the H. J. Heinz Company, was riding on an elevated railway in New York City in 1896 when he saw an "advertising card" for shoes that read "21 Styles." Heinz was taken with the idea of using a number to promote his company and started counting in his head the variety of products his company produced. He easily counted more than sixty but he kept coming back to the number 57. There was something special about the number seven. "Seven, seven," quoted E. D. McCafferty in his book *Henry J. Heinz: a Biography*. "There are so many illustrations of the psychological influence of that figure and of its alluring significance to people of all ages and races that '58 Varieties' or '59 Varieties' did not appeal at all to me as being equally strong." That's why "57 Varieties" is still the company's motto.

A Slave to Fashion

We are led to believe, in our abbreviated versions of history, that all slave-holding states seceded from the Union during the Civil War, or else they gave up the practice of slavery. But that's just not true. Kentucky, Missouri, Maryland, and Delaware remained in the Union but continued to allow citizens to own slaves. They were referred to as "border states" and were joined by West Virginia when it was admitted to the Union in 1863 (after it split from the northwestern counties of Virginia after Virginia seceded from the Union). Once again, this demonstrates that the Civil War was anything but black and white.

Curtain Call

On June 13, 1932, twenty-four-year-old actress Peg Entwistle signed a contract for a one-picture deal with RKO Studios and reported early in July to shoot her part as "Hazel Cousins" in *Thirteen Women*. The film received poor feedback from test screenings, and the studio re-edited the film, greatly reducing Entwistle's screen time. On September 16, 1932, Entwistle climbed up the giant "H" in the famous Hollywood sign (which read Hollywoodland, at that time) and jumped to her death. In a cruel twist of fate, Entwistle's uncle opened a letter addressed to the dead actress from the Beverly Hills Playhouse, mailed the day before she jumped. The letter was an offer for Entwistle to play the lead role in a theatrical production in which her character commits suicide.

There were more than 46,000 write-in votes for Edward "Ted" Kennedy for U.S. senator in 1962. Which isn't stupid in and of itself—until you discover that the voters lived in Connecticut, while Kennedy was running in Massachusetts.

Behind Every Good Man

On October 2, 1919, President Woodrow Wilson suffered a severe stroke, and he was soon bedridden and incapacitated. The president's wife, Edith Bolling Galt Wilson, did more than just take control of the president's recovery; she also took control of the presidency. She would bring important papers to her husband under the guise of explaining them to him, but what she was actually doing was making presidential decisions in his place. For the next six weeks, she was the true power behind the presidency, although she claimed, "I, myself, never made a single decision regarding the disposition of public affairs. The only decision that was mine was what was important and what was not." She has been labeled "the secret president" and even "the first female president of the United States." Mrs. Wilson was both criticized and ridiculed by many as the "presidentress" who was running a "petticoat government."

Suffering Suffragette

There are two women who ran for president who shared a very unusual situation in history. Even though they ran for the office, they couldn't vote for themselves or anyone else, for that matter. Victoria Claflin Woodhull ran on the National Radical Reform ticket in 1872, and Belva Ann Bennett Lockwood ran on the National Equal Rights ticket in 1884 and 1888. Why could they run for the presidency but not vote in the election? Because both women ran before the Nineteenth Amendment to the Constitution was ratified in 1920—giving women the right to vote.

Getting to the Bottom of the Constitution

The Twenty-Fifth Amendment authorizing the vice president to take over the presidency if the president is temporarily incapacitated is relatively new, having been enacted in 1967. As of this printing, the amendment has been used only three times:

- On July 13, 1985, President Ronald Reagan underwent surgery to remove cancerous polyps from his colon and Vice President George H. W. Bush took over the presidency.

- On June 29, 2002, Vice President Dick Cheney temporarily took over the presidency when President George W. Bush had a colonoscopy that required sedation.

- On July 21, 2007, President George W. Bush had to undergo the same procedure and Dick Cheney, once again, took over the Oval Office.

I'm glad the Twenty-Fifth Amendment filled in all the cracks in the transference of presidential powers.

Strange Interlude

Future Pulitzer prize–winning playwright and Nobel laureate in literature Eugene O'Neill attended Princeton University during the 1907–1908 term, but he was kicked out after his freshman year. He was expelled, not only for poor grades, but also for allegedly being drunk and disorderly at a reception held by the university president, future President of the United States Woodrow Wilson.

E very U.S. president with a beard has been a Republican. In case you're curious, the five bearded presidents were Abraham Lincoln, Ulysses S. Grant, Rutherford Hayes, James Garfield, and Benjamin Harrison.

That's Sort of Weird

On September 11, 2002, the first anniversary of the September 11 terrorist attacks, the numbers that popped up for the New York Lottery were 9-1-1. So what were the chances of those three numbers coming up on the anniversary of the attacks in the same city in which the attacks took place? Seems like it might be astronomical, but it's actually the same as any three-number combinations: 1 out of 1,000. Sorry, conspiracy theorists.

Notorious Wild West "peacekeeper" James Butler "Wild Bill" Hickok shot only two people while presiding over Abilene, Texas; one of them was another policeman.

Just for the Record

In the American lexicon there are some words that don't seem to make sense anymore because their original meanings have been lost. Take, for example, the use of the word "album" for a vinyl record. When records spun at 78 RPM, they could only hold four to five minutes of music per side. So you needed several records if you were listening to a symphony or an opera. The records were packaged in brown paper sleeves that fanned out from inside a leather-bound book that resembled a photo album. Soon, any long-playing record was called an album whether it came in a set or by itself.

Don't Have a Cow, Man I

Mickey Mouse is usually a moral, upright do-gooder with a heart of gold. So why would one of his cartoons ever be banned? Well, one was in Ohio in 1932. The cartoon, *The Shindig*, showed Clarabelle Cow, the first cartoon in which she's identified by name, in the stable reading a book titled *Three Weeks*. So what's the big deal? For one, when her boyfriend Horace Horsecollar knocks on the door, Clarabelle gets up and dresses, so she was technically naked while she was reading the book. The second big deal was that *Three Weeks* was written by Elinor Glyn, a British novelist and scriptwriter who pioneered mass-market women's erotic fiction and also coined the use of the word "It" as a euphemism for sex appeal (1920s motion picture sex starlet Clara Bow was called "The It Girl"). *Three Weeks* was deemed obscene, banned in Canada in 1907, and condemned by religious leaders in the United States. How it came to be used in a Walt Disney cartoon remains a mystery to this day.

All in the Family

George W. Bush is related to two former presidents: his father, George H. W. Bush (1989–1993), and his fourth cousin five times removed—Franklin Pierce, president from 1853 to 1857. Barbara Pierce Bush is the only woman in U.S. history to be the wife of one president, mother to another, and fourth cousin of another.

A Needling Rumor

You might not know the name Elizabeth Griscom Ross, but if I called her Betsy Ross, you'd say she's the woman who designed and sewed the first flag. But sewing the flag is a yarn created by Betsy's grandson, William Canby. Canby first mentioned the moment in March 1870 (thirty-six years after his grandmother had died) before a meeting of the Historical Society of Pennsylvania, claiming Betsy told him about the first flag while on her deathbed when he was eleven. There is proof that Betsy had sewn "ship's colors" for the Pennsylvania Navy in May 1777 but nothing whatsoever that supports one of the most beloved rumors in American history.

After Canby's death, a book called *The Evolution of the American Flag* was published in 1909, and it used Canby's claim of the Betsy Ross story as fact. The misinformation spread from there.

Never a Twain Shall Meet

There are a few things most people know about Mark Twain. One, he is one of the greatest American authors in history. Two, his real name was Samuel Langhorne Clemens. And three, he got his name from the traditional call of Mississippi boaters who announced "Mark Twain" (the second mark on a leadline used to calculate the river's depth) that indicated two fathoms (twelve feet)—a safe depth for boats to travel. The first two are correct but Clemens didn't get his name from a nautical term— he Shanghaid it. Captain Isaiah Sellers, a river news correspondent for the New Orleans *Picayune*, used the name Mark Twain first. When Sellers died in 1863, Clemens began using the name as his own. He explained this personally in a letter, stating, "as he [Sellers] could no longer need that signature, I laid violent hands upon it without asking permission of the proprietor's remains. That is the history of the nom de plume I bear."

Marx on Our Past

The Pilgrims have come to symbolize the heart of the American spirit. But when they first arrived in Plymouth in 1620, they established their community in a most un-American way—they were communists. Under the Mayflower Compact, the Pilgrims attempted to create a just and equal society; whatever they produced was put into a common warehouse, with each individual getting one equal share. All the land, buildings, and end product were owned communally. How well did it work? Well, you don't see too many Pilgrims walking around these days, do you? Actually, it only worked for a year or two, and then they changed to that most American economic structure—capitalism.

Leave the Light On for Me

Most cities have what is commonly referred to as a red-light district; a place where prostitutes ply their trade. So why is it called a red-light district? The usually agreed-upon answer is that when railway workers visited "women of the night," they would hang their red lanterns outside the brothels so they could be found if they were needed.

Robert McNamara, U.S. secretary of defense
from 1961 to 1968, had a very strange middle name:
Strange. He got his middle name "Strange"
from his mother's maiden name.

The First Real American President

The first president to be born a citizen of the United States was number eight, Martin Van Buren. He was born on December 5, 1782, six years after the signing of the Declaration of Independence. Because all previous presidents had been born before the American Revolution, they were actually British subjects.

❧

Civil War Union General William Tecumseh Sherman, named at birth for the notorious Indian chief, added William as his first name.

The Peanut Nut

One of the most shining examples of sibling embarrassment for any president had to be Jimmy Carter's brother, Billy. Billy personified the beer-gutted, beer-swigging hillbilly stereotype, and he was consistently making the news. Once it was for judging and participating in a world championship belly flop competition; another time he even urinated on an airport tarmac while awaiting a delegation of Libyans he was hosting. He even went so far as to accept a $220,000 loan from Libya (at that time, an enemy of the United States), which propelled him once again into the spotlight as the key subject in a federal investigation.

❧

When Billy Carter was asked why his brother Jimmy
didn't try to control his behavior, Billy said,
"I'd tell him to kiss my ass."

A Civil Union

One would think that the Puritans believed in the purity and sanctity of marriage—and they did; they just didn't think the marriage ceremony should be religious in nature. In fact, in 1647 the Puritans in New England actually outlawed the preaching of wedding ceremonies (the year before they mandated that all wedding ceremonies be conducted by a civil magistrate). The rationale was that the Puritans believed marriage was a government institution, not a religious one. Before the end of the century, however, the Puritans vowed that it was all right for weddings to take place in a church and allowed both ministers and justices of the peace to perform the ceremony.

Bad Timing

Financial executive and the builder of the Empire State Building, John Jacob Raskob, wrote an article for the *Ladies' Home Journal* entitled "Everybody Ought to Be Rich"—just a month before the stock market crashed in October 1929.

A Legend in His Own Mind

Legendary Wild West gunman Bat Masterson (William Barclay Masterson, 1853–1921) has been considered a notorious killer for years. The stories of his gun-slinging skills are legendary, and legends they are. It has been reported that Masterson killed twenty-seven men, but according to Robert DeArment's thoroughly researched biography, he is only credited with killing one person.

Shooting Blanks

It is common knowledge that the military purposely puts saltpeter in the food of enlisted men to curb their sexual appetite. It's well known, all right—but it's a well-known falsehood. There's no proof that potassium nitrate (known as saltpeter) has any effect on the libido, one way or the other. One theory as to why this rumor started is simply because the name saltpeter sounds like it might have some negative effect on a service member.

Stupid History

Tough Love

In colonial Connecticut, the adage "spare the rod and spoil the child" was taken seriously. George Brinley's book *The Laws of Connecticut* shows just how seriously they took this advice to heart. "If any Childe or Children above fifteen years old, and of sufficient understanding, shall Curse or Smite their natural Father or Mother, he or they shall be put to death, unless it can be sufficiently testified, that the Parents have been unchristianly negligent in the education of such Children."

Let's Make a Deal

Here's how it went: Spiro Agnew resigned after bribery allegations had surfaced. Richard Nixon appointed Gerald Ford to take Agnew's place as vice president. When Richard Nixon resigned after Watergate, Gerald Ford took over as president of the United States, and he appointed Nelson Rockefeller as his vice president. Shortly after taking the reins of power, Gerald Ford granted Richard Nixon a full pardon for any crimes he may have committed in the Watergate case. Then Ford lobbied Congress to award former President Nixon $850,000 to cover expenses while he made the transition from the White House to civilian life—a compromise was reached and Nixon was given $200,000.

Ford considered the sum of $850,000 to be fair because the Presidential Transition Act of 1963 provides ex-presidents (who complete their full term in office) funds not to exceed $900,000 to cover their expenses during the six-month transition period.

A Big Wig

Beautiful elegant dresses, silk stockings, the newest fashions from France, and high-heeled boots to die for were the customary clothes of the governor of New York who served from 1702 to 1708. What's the big deal, you might ask? Well, he wasn't a female—he was a notorious transvestite named Lord Cornbury (Edward Hyde) and not surprisingly a favorite of Queen Anne. Lord Cornbury had long, luscious nails, wore his hair in the most fashionable coif, and was frequently seen parading around the grounds of the governor's mansion. And you thought politicians today were a real drag.

Herbert Hoover was the only president to turn his entire salary over to charity.

Going Down

In 1975 Congress modernized the elevators in the Capitol building, changing them from the old-fashioned manually operated ones to the new push-button type. So the need for elevator operators was eliminated, right? This is Congress, remember. It was decided that the elevator operators would stay on the government payroll and continue their new duties—pushing the buttons on automatic elevators.

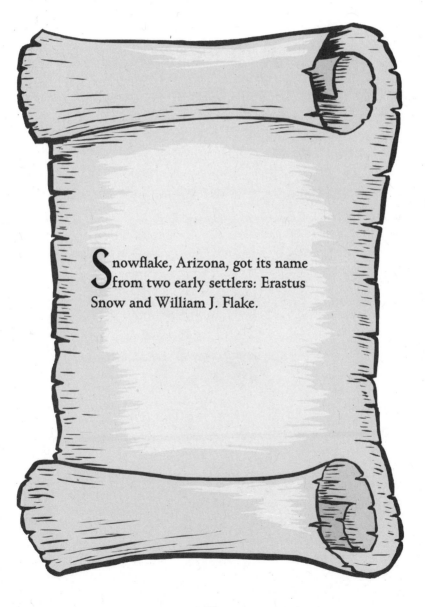

Snowflake, Arizona, got its name from two early settlers: Erastus Snow and William J. Flake.

Representin'

The first African American elected to the U.S. Senate was Hiram Rhodes Revels, who represented Mississippi in 1870 and 1871, during Reconstruction. In an ironic twist, the man who occupied the seat before Revel was Jefferson Davis, president of the Confederacy.

*I*n 1792, New York Governor George Clinton basically stole the governor's race from John Jay, Alexander Hamilton's handpicked candidate, simply by declaring the votes of three counties invalid and announcing himself the winner. Clinton was New York's first and longest-serving governor, having been re-elected six times.

A Bad First Act

Most Americans imagine that our founding fathers were big on liberty, free speech, and all that other stuff—but not during the administration of John Adams. In 1798, Adams signed four bills into law called the Alien and Sedition Acts that were supposed to protect American interests against foreign intrusion during our undeclared naval war with France. One of the bills, the Sedition Act, made it a crime to publish "false, scandalous, and malicious writing against" the government or its officials. So the Federalists in Congress could jail anyone who criticized anything the government did. More than twenty Republican newspaper editors were indicted and most were sent to jail.

Thomas Jefferson was vice president during the enforcement of the Alien and Sedition Acts, and he stopped signing his letters out of fear that postal clerks would search his mail looking for evidence to charge him with treason.

Remember It Correctly

There are a few things that come to mind when the state of Texas is mentioned: big hats, longhorns, and the Battle of the Alamo. When the Mexican army was taken by surprise at the short-lived (approximately eighteen minutes) Battle of San Jacinto, "Remember the Alamo" was the battle cry of the Americans. But what was the Battle of the Alamo? Did Mexican forces invade the United States? No, it was just the opposite. Mexican President Antonio López de Santa Anna was attempting to retake the province after an army of Texan settlers and adventurers had driven Mexican troops off their own land.

In Congress Assembled

The Continental Congress, which met in three incarnations from 1774 to 1789, was very different from the Congress we have today. They actually got things done. But despite having to deal with highly important matters (establishing a country isn't as easy as it sounds), they still had time for trivial matters—and I'm not talking about giving post offices celebrity names. During one session, the Continental Congress spent hours debating whether one James Whitehead should receive $64 in compensation for feeding British prisoners; they decided in his favor. Then there was the debate over paying a wagon master $222.60 for transporting army supplies to Dobbs Ferry, New York, and Cambridge, Massachusetts. After several hours of heated debate, they decided to pay him, too.

Off Key

Contrary to what most people believe, Francis Scott Key didn't write the song *The Star-Spangled Banner*. He wrote a poem called *Defense of Fort McHenry* from which the lyrics of *The Star-Spangled Banner* were taken.

❦

Richard M. Nixon was the first president to be nominated for a Grammy award. He was nominated for Best Spoken Word Award for an album made from the soundtrack of his television interview with David Frost.

Sub-Standard

Submarine warfare is usually thought of in terms of German U2s and the well-documented battles during World War II. But the first submarine used in warfare came much earlier. In fact, the Americans used the first submarine during the War of Independence. A sub was invented by Yale graduate David Bushnell, and was used only once. The small wooden-framed, oval-shaped vessel (called "the Turtle") only had enough room for one person and enough oxygen for a half-hour submersion. On September 6, 1776, First Sergeant Ezra Lee propelled the small submarine close to the British warship HMS *Eagle* and attempted to attach a bomb to the hull of the ship with an iron screw. Unfortunately, the ship had a copper-sheathed hull that the screw could not penetrate. Even though George Washington was an enthusiastic supporter of the Turtle and submarine technology, the Continental Congress cut off all funding for the project.

The Good Ole Days—
Part I

Most people think our forefathers were gracious and eloquent men of class and honor—not like the members of Congress we have today. Well, I hate to burst the bubble, but here are verbatim excerpts from the *Historical Summary of Conduct Cases in the House of Representatives* by the Committee on Standards of Official Conduct:

- Representative Matthew Lyon (VT) (1798) "Disorderly behavior" (spat on Rep. Roger Griswold after an exchange of insults), (Jan. 30, 1798); charge added of "gross indecency of language in his defense before this House" (Feb. 8, 1798).

- Representative Roger Griswold (CT) and Representative Matthew Lyon (VT) "Disorderly behavior" (Rep. Griswold assaulted Representative Lyon with a "stout cane" on the House floor before the House was in session and Rep. Lyon responded by attacking Representative Griswold with fireplace tongs), (Feb. 15, 1798).

Peal and Crack

The Liberty Bell was cast at the Whitechapel Bell Foundry in London, England, and delivered to Philadelphia in late August to early September 1752 via the ship *Hibernia*. In March of 1753, the bell was hung from temporary scaffolding in the square outside the State House, and it cracked when it was first rung. It was repaired and recast several times, but the crack kept coming back.

Eli Whitney technically didn't invent the cotton gin; he borrowed the idea from an earlier invention and improved upon it. The "gin" part of the name was short for "engine."

Etymologically Speaking

During the debate over the Missouri Compromise of 1820, Felix Walker, congressman from Buncombe County, North Carolina, stood up in the House and said he wanted "to make a speech for Buncombe" even though the matter up for debate was irrelevant to Walker's district. His rant was so long-winded and disjointed that a new word, "buncombe" (later respelled "bunkum"), was coined. It was defined as "Speech-making for the gratification of constituents, or to gain public applause" or "nonsense," and from that word we get the more modern derivative, "bunk."

Deal or No Deal

A loyalist spy learned that George Washington and his small Continental Army had secretly crossed the Delaware River earlier on the day after Christmas in 1776 and were headed toward Trenton, New Jersey. The spy arrived at the home of merchant Abraham Hunt where the leader of the Hessian army, Colonel Johann Rall, was drinking and playing cards. The colonel refused to break from his game of cards and demanded the spy hand over the written message, which he promptly put in his vest pocket without reading. Colonel Rall was awakened the next day to the sound of musket fire and, having no time to organize or rally his troops, suffered a crushing defeat at the hands of Washington's army. He also suffered two wounds that led to his eventual death the following day and gave the Continental Army its first victory over the British.

Grand Old Flag

When Vermont and Kentucky came into the Union on March 4, 1791, and June 1, 1792, respectively, Congress altered the standard flag of thirteen stars and thirteen stripes and adopted a flag of fifteen stars and fifteen stripes. In 1818, after Tennessee, Ohio, Louisiana, and Indiana joined the Union, Congress knew that the flag would soon look like a quilt if they kept adding stripes for each new state. They decided to revert back to the original thirteen stripes and to simply add a star for every new state.

Andrew Jackson was the first president to be handed a baby to kiss during his campaign. He refused to kiss the infant, and instead he handed the baby over to his secretary of war.

No, No, Sirhan Sirhan

On May 10, 1982, convicted killer Sirhan Sirhan told a parole board, "I sincerely believe that if Robert Kennedy were alive today, I believe he would not countenance singling me out for this kind of treatment. I think he would be among the first to say that, however horrible the deed I committed fourteen years ago was, that it should not be the cause for denying me equal treatment under the laws of this country." Sirhan is serving life in prison for the June 5, 1968, assassination of Robert Kennedy.

❧

The first child born on the *Mayflower*
was named Oceanus Hopkins.

Cabin Fever

President William Henry Harrison, who served only thirty-two days in office before his death from blood poisoning complicated by pneumonia and jaundice, campaigned as a candidate of humble beginnings. He was touted as having been born in a log cabin, and Harrison himself made references to his "log cabin home." But he was actually born in a two-and-a-half-story red brick mansion located on a large plantation on the James River in Virginia. The only log cabin to which he could lay claim was one that happened to be on his property and that one he most definitely never lived in.

No Bull

There is a much believed but erroneous story that Sitting Bull killed Lieutenant Colonel George Armstrong Custer during the Battle of the Little Bighorn on June 25, 1876. Sitting Bull didn't fight in the battle because he was simply too old at the time, but he did serve as his tribe's holy man. His earlier premonitions that all his enemies would be delivered into his hands came true after Custer's Last Stand.

Abraham Lincoln was the first and only president to receive a patent. Patent #6469 was a very complex device, much like car safety air-bags of today, that incorporated chambers of air. But Lincoln's invention was much grander and was designed to help heavy ships pass through shallow water.

Cut to the Chase

In 1903, when the Gillette Company started selling safety razors with disposable blades, they were shocked when hundreds of men complained that the razors didn't work. It was soon discovered that the stubby disgruntled customers weren't removing the wrapping from around the blades before they put them into the razor.

Amerian author Sherwood Anderson died in Panama at the age of sixty-four from peritonitis. The infection resulted when the author accidentally swallowed a piece of a toothpick embedded in a martini olive.

Doesn't Fall Far from the Tree

When one thinks of outrageous American folk heroes it doesn't take long for the names Paul Bunyan and Johnny Appleseed to pop up. Johnny Appleseed was a real person, but old Paul was a myth. Johnny Appleseed, born John Chapman (1774–1845), was an eccentric American nurseryman who introduced the apple to large parts of mainly Ohio, but also to Indiana and Illinois. Appleseed planted orchards and then turned their care over to neighbors who sold the apples and gave some of the profit to Appleseed. He would usually give it all away to charity. The image of him going barefoot is true—he never wore shoes even in winter—and it's possible that he wore a pot on his head because Appleseed remained a wanderer his entire life and carried all his meager belongings with him.

Every Vote Counts

Before he died on October 18, 1931, Thomas Edison, "The Wizard of Menlo Park," held 1,093 U.S. patents. His first patent, granted in 1868, was for a vote counter intended to speed up the election process in Congress. Members of Congress, however, rejected the invention because they felt that, somehow, slowly tabulating votes was to their advantage.

A correspondent for the *New York Tribune* who reported on politics in Europe during the Civil War later became infamous not as a newspaperman but as the father of modern communism—Karl Marx.

Look at the Flip Side

Even though American money bears the motto "In God We Trust," which Treasury Secretary Salmon P. Chase had placed on the two-cent coin in 1864, not everyone has thought it an enlightened move. In 1907, President Theodore Roosevelt wrote to a friend saying, "It seems to me eminently unwise to cheapen such a motto by use on coins, just as it would be to cheapen it by use on postage stamps, or in advertisements." However, the courts have consistently upheld the use of the motto even though it has historically had opposition from constitutionalists (citing the First Amendment, "Congress shall make no law respecting an establishment of religion").

❧

On July 30, 1956, President Dwight D. Eisenhower
declared "In God We Trust" the national motto
of the United States.

Going Off Half-Cocked

Robert Shurtleff (1760–1827) was a former indentured servant who enlisted in the Continental Army in 1782 and fought with the Fourth Massachusetts. Fellow soldiers gave Shurtleff the nickname Molly because of his inability to grow facial hair. Shurtleff was treated for a wound to the head but didn't tell the doctor about being shot in the thigh and tried to treat the wound personally. After being struck down with a fever, it was soon discovered that facial hair wasn't the only thing "Molly" hadn't grown—you see, Robert Shurtleff was actually a woman named Deborah Sampson. Sampson was discharged in 1783 and was the only woman to officially fight in the Revolutionary War. She was given a small pension, and, in 1802, she became one of the first American women to speak on a lecture tour. In 1838 Congress granted her heirs a full military pension.

The Original Benedict Arnold

How did the best general and most accomplished leader in the Continental Army become America's best known traitor? It started when the Continental Congress passed over Benedict Arnold for promotion even though if it hadn't been for his heroic contributions to the American Revolution we would all speak with an English accent. Arnold became despondent with what he believed was an affront to his honor and accomplishments (other generals took credit for a number of his deeds). Then Congress investigated his accounts because of his personal debts, and he became the target of political adversaries. He was charged with corruption, and he opposed America's new alliance with France. So when he was given command of the American fort at West Point, New York, he had had enough and decided to change sides.

Up, Up, and Away

It is sometimes reported that one year after Charles Lindbergh flew solo across the Atlantic Ocean in May 1927, Amelia Earhart became the first woman to do the same. Well, she did fly across the Atlantic in June 1928 but only as a passenger—she wasn't trained to fly on "instruments" and did not pilot the aircraft. When interviewed after landing, she said, "I was just baggage, like a sack of potatoes." She added, " . . . maybe someday I'll try it alone." And in May 1932 she did just that.

To her credit, in January 1935, Amelia Earhart became the first person to fly solo from Honolulu, Hawaii, to Oakland, California.

❦

In 1875, James Stephen Hogg, the first native-born Texan to become the state's governor, named his daughter: Ima.

356

A Tall Tale

In 1869, while digging a well at an upstate New York farm just outside the town of Cardiff, workers found what appeared to be the petrified body of a man, but not just any man—a ten-foot-tall giant. When New York cigar maker George Hull, who had hired the workers, found out about their discovery, he began touring with the petrified body, which was known as the Cardiff Giant. He charged people 50 cents to see it. P. T. Barnum, who knew a good thing when he saw it, offered to buy the giant from Hull, and when Hull refused, he simply created his own giant and put it on display. He then sued Hull, declaring the original to be a fake. During the trial, Hull admitted the giant was an elaborate hoax, carved from gypsum and washed with sulfuric acid to make it look old. He created the hoax for two reasons: first, because he had an argument with a fundamentalist preacher concerning the "giants in the Earth" mentioned in the Bible; and, second, to make a bunch of money off the rubes of the Earth.

❧

In 1938, *Time* magazine named as its Man of the Year—
Adolf Hitler.

The End of His Rope

In 1872, criminals Patrick Morrissey, convicted of stabbing his mother to death, and Jack Gaffney were hanged by the neck until dead by the sheriff of Erie County, New York, who had the nickname The Buffalo Hangman. In 1885, the notorious hangman was referred to by another name, President Grover Cleveland.

Richard Nixon was the only person ever elected twice to both the office of president and the office of vice president. He also holds the less distinguished honor of being the only president ever to resign.

How to Afford a Ford

We've all heard the infamous remark made by Henry Ford concerning the variety of colors for his Model T Ford: "Any color so long as it's black." But what most people don't know is that the car originally was painted green with a red stripe. However, it was only after an engineer discovered that black paint dried faster and therefore would speed up the assembly line process (it was cheaper, too) that Ford made the decision to paint all of his cars black.

No one knows what Christopher Columbus really looked like because he never sat for a painting.

Washington's Embarrassing Discharge

It's highly likely that the father of our country wasn't able to father a child by anybody. Even though George Washington claimed that he always wanted children, he and Martha never conceived. Martha, who had four children in seven years during her previous marriage, obviously wasn't at fault, so that leaves only one possibility: Washington had a monumental problem.

John Kennedy, at age forty-three, was not the youngest president of the United States. The youngest president was Theodore Roosevelt at forty-two. Kennedy, however, was the youngest man to be elected president—Roosevelt became president after McKinley died from an assassin's bullet on September 14, 1901.

Not Whole Cloth

One thing about the Declaration of Independence that isn't widely known is that Jefferson had to present the document to Congress for approval. Congress debated the document and, of course, made changes. In total, Congress made eighty-six revisions to Jefferson's masterpiece, eliminating 480 of his words. The most striking changes were that Congress removed all references to "the execrable commerce"—slavery.

That's Snot a Good Name!

In 1962 the city council of Burleson, Texas, officially changed the name of Town Creek to Little Booger Creek. In 2001, when city managers wanted to apply for a federal grant for a creek-side hike and bike trail, they decided to change the name back to Town Creek so the paperwork wouldn't have a "booger" on it.

No American president has been an only child. Although, technically, Franklin D. Roosevelt had a younger half brother, Gerald Ford had four half brothers and two half sisters, and Bill Clinton has one younger half brother.

Tag, You're It!

There's a myth that circulated for years concerning government dog tags issued to United States Army personnel during World War II. This particularly morbid myth concerns the notches on both sides of the tags. It is rumored that the notches were placed between the teeth of a dead soldier, and then the mouth was kicked shut, ensuring the proper identification of the corpse. But the real answer is that the notches are there to hold the tag in place on the embossing machine. The new dog tags, which use a different embossing machine, don't have the notches.

You Say Tomato and I Say Tomato

It wasn't until the early 1800s that Americans began eating tomatoes, even though they are native to North America. It was believed that they were poisonous, because the tomato is related to the sometimes deadly Nightshade family. However, tomatoes were grown as decorative plants and commonly referred to as "love apples." Thomas Jefferson was a fan of the tomato (or "tomatas," as he called them in his journal) and grew them abundantly in his garden despite their unpopularity. Thomas Mann Randolph, Jefferson's son-in-law, in his 1824 speech before the Albemarle Agricultural Society, mentioned that tomatoes were relatively unknown ten years earlier, but by 1824 everyone was eating them because it was believed they "kept one's blood pure in the heat of summer."

Details, Details, Details

President Martin Van Buren wrote his autobiography during 1862, the last year of his life, finally dictating it shortly before he died. But for some reason, Van Buren overlooked one aspect of his life—the fact that he had been married. He never mentioned his wife, Hannah Hoes, in the book at all.

❦

Samuel Mudd, the doctor who treated the broken ankle of Lincoln's assassin, John Wilkes Booth, received a presidential pardon in 1869 by Ulysses S. Grant. Contrary to some beliefs, the phrase "Your name is mud!" didn't originate with Dr. Mudd.

A Taxing Situation

Taxes and America have had a long past. In fact, the fight against "taxation without representation" helped drive us to become a free country in the first place. So when did we decide that taxing ourselves was okay? It started in 1861 when Congress passed the first income tax law as an emergency measure to fund the Civil War. In 1872, Congress repealed the income tax law but twenty-two years later, after complaints about excessive tariffs, Congress again approved an income tax. In 1895, the U.S. Supreme Court ruled that the income tax law was unconstitutional, and it was revoked. So what to do when a law is unconstitutional? Change the Constitution. Which is exactly what was done when the Sixteenth Amendment to the Constitution was enacted in 1913.

Not in a Box, Not with a Fox

Twenty-three New York publishers rejected Theodor Geisel's first book before one decided it was worth printing. *And To Think That I Saw It On Mulberry Street* went on to sell millions of copies and started the career of the beloved children's author, Dr. Seuss.

❧

During the American Revolution, many brides did not wear white gowns during their wedding; as a sign of rebellion, they wore red.

Cold, Harsh Cash

A week before Christmas 1777, George Washington and his Continental Army established camp at Valley Forge, Pennsylvania, for the winter, remaining there until June 1778. It's true that as many as 2,000 men died during those six months, but it wasn't because of the weather. The close quarters were a breeding ground for typhus, typhoid, dysentery, and pneumonia, but the main killer was mismanagement and indifference. Pennsylvania farmers elected to sell their produce to the British instead of the new United States because they trusted the English sterling over the recently minted American money.

Apollos Rivoire and Deborah Hitchbourn were French Huguenots who moved to Boston after being driven from France. In America, Apollos Rivoire changed his name to Paul Rivoire, and then to Paul Revere— the name he gave to his first son.

I'll Drink to That

The idea that it was against the law to drink alcoholic beverages during Prohibition (1920–1933) is patently untrue. You were free to drink as much booze as you wanted so as long as the alcohol had been purchased prior to the enactment of the Eighteenth Amendment. The National Prohibition Act, commonly referred to as the "Volstead Act," established the legal definition of intoxicating liquor as well as providing for enforcement of Prohibition. While the manufacture, sale, and transport of alcohol were illegal under Section 29 of the Volstead Act, it did allow for homemade wine and hard cider from fruit (but no beer)—up to 200 gallons per year.

Don't Fence Me In

In 1626, the Dutch purchased "New Amsterdam" from the Native Americans, and soon tensions began to mount. In 1653, Dutch Governor Peter Stuyvesant ordered walls to be erected between the Hudson and East River to protect the town from marauding Indians. Originally, they were basic plank fences, but as tensions mounted, the walls became taller and stronger. In 1669, the British tore down the walls after having taken over New Amsterdam five years earlier, and they renamed it New York. The walls are gone, but they live on in the name given to the street that ran alongside them—Wall Street.

Breaking the Rules

John H. Eaton, U.S. senator from Tennessee, was the youngest senator ever elected. He was twenty-eight years old when he was sworn in on November 16, 1818, even though the minimum age requirement set forth in the United States Constitution is thirty years.

John Sedgwick, a Union general during the Civil War, was killed during the Battle of Spotsylvania Court House on May 9, 1864, while watching Confederate troops. His last words were, "They couldn't hit an elephant at this distance."

It's the Alabaster Plaster

Many of us have heard the story that the White House got its name because, after the British burned it in August 1814 during the War of 1812, it was painted white to hide the damage. And if that were true it wouldn't be in this book. Massachusetts Congressman Abijah Bigelow wrote to a colleague on March 18, 1812 (three months before the United States declared war on Britain on June 18, 1812), "There is much trouble at the White House, as we call it." The White House has been called, at various times in history, the "President's House," the "President's Palace," and the "Executive Mansion." In 1901 President Theodore Roosevelt officially named it the White House.

Their Native Tongue

The first Bible printed in America (the New Testament in 1661 and the full text in 1663) was not the King James version, nor was it written in English, French, or German. It was written in the Massachusetts Indian dialect—Algonquin. The "Algonquin Bible," or "Mamusse Wunneetupanatamwe up-Biblum God naneeswe Nukkone Testament kah wonk Wusku Testament," as it is technically known, was translated by John Eliot and published in Cambridge, Massachusetts.

In 1978, President Jimmy Carter, the first Southerner elected to the presidency following the Civil War, restored U.S. citizenship to Jefferson Davis, president of the Confederate States of America.

Stupid History

Eat My Shorts, Man

"Baghdad Betty," an Iraqi government propaganda broadcaster, warned American soldiers during the first Gulf War that "Bart Simpson is making love to your wife." The story, which ran rampant during the early 1990s, was supposed to be the modern equivalent of the infamous but fictitious propagandist Tokyo Rose. According to a 1991 article in the *Toronto Star*, the rumor started as a monologue by Johnny Carson on his August 22, 1990, broadcast of *The Tonight Show*. But in the original monologue the men making love to American soldiers' wives were Tom Selleck, Tom Cruise, and Homer Simpson. The story evolved to Bart Simpson, probably because it made the Iraqis seem stupid and easy to conquer.

It wasn't until the early 1990s
that women were allowed to wear pants
on the Senate floor.

Mentioning Her Unmentionables

On August 8, 1840, a Comanche war party attacked the port
town of Linnville, Texas, burning, looting, and rampaging. Most
of the settlers escaped in their small boats, but Juliet Watts and her
husband, Hugh, ran back to their house to save their possessions. The
Comanche killed Hugh and kidnapped Juliet. Days later, as the retreating
Indians were attacked and defeated by a posse at the Battle of Plum
Creek, Mrs. Watts was shot in the breast with an arrow. One thing
stood between the arrow and certain death for Mrs. Watts—her corset.

The fake gun John Dillinger used to escape from the Lake County Jail in Crown Point, Indiana, on March 3, 1934, was carved from wood—not soap.

Back Too Soon?

John Scott Harrison (1804–1878) was an Ohio representative and the only man to be both the father and son of U.S. presidents. His father was William Henry Harrison (ninth president) and his son was Benjamin Harrison (twenty-third president). His body was stolen by gravediggers and sold to the Medical College of Ohio in Cincinnati for use as a training cadaver. It was eventually recovered and re-interred.

Stupid History

That's Too Baaaad

In 1918 during World War I, President Woodrow Wilson allowed sheep to graze on the White House lawn to replace the gardeners who had volunteered to serve in the armed forces. He was able to raise $52,823 for the Red Cross by shearing the sheep and selling their wool.

The initials "LBJ" didn't just stand for Lyndon Baines Johnson. They actually stood for every member of the Johnson family: Lady Bird Johnson, his wife; their daughters, Lynda Bird Johnson and Luci Baines Johnson; and the family dog, Little Beagle Johnson.

Got You under My Spell

Theodore Roosevelt never backed down from a fight even when his opponent was Merriam-Webster. Roosevelt was a believer in simplifying the spelling of hundreds of English words, particularly eliminating silent vowels. He ordered the U.S. Government Printing Office to change the spelling of 300 specific words in all government publications. Some of the spelling changes didn't fare so well: "kissed" became "kist," "addressed" became "addrest," "blushed" became "blusht," "crossed" became "crost," and "gypsy" became "gipsy." The "s" was exchanged for a "z" in "exorcize" and "compromize," and the "e" was kicked out of the word "whisky." When Congress came back into session they debated the issue and voted against Roosevelt and his "bully" language. One word change that eventually resurfaced was the spelling of "through" to "thru."

The Devil and
Webster's Dictionary

Henry Watterson, editor of the *Louisville Courier-Journal,* amused or angered over Theodore Roosevelt's tampering with the English language, wrote: "Nuthing escapes Mr. Rucevelt. No subject is tu hi fr him to takl, nor tu lo for him tu notis. He makes tretis without the consent of the Senit. He inforces such laws as meet his approval, and fales to se those that du not soot him. He now assales the English langgwidg, constitutes himself a sort of French Academy, and will reform the spelling in a way tu soot himself."

✺

In 1937, Gertrude Stein, an American writer who spent most of her life in France, proposed that Adolf Hitler receive the Nobel Peace Prize.

Mother Knows Best

At age fourteen, George Washington received word from his half-brother Lawrence that the British Royal Navy was seeking a new midshipman. Washington knew a spot in His Majesty's Navy would mean a lifetime of adventure as well as a wonderful career. His mother, Mary, who ruled over George most of his life, seriously considered the plan and at one point nearly gave George her blessing. But after some soul searching, Mary decided that George should stay with her and not dedicate his life to the sea. We should all be thankful for Mary Washington's decision because had she allowed George to take that appointment in 1746, he would have been fighting on the side of the British during the American Revolution!

Cashing Out

When Grover Cleveland was drafted into the Union Army during the Civil War, he did what any other red-blooded American would do: He paid a substitute $150 to take his place. What Cleveland did was completely legal under the terms of the Conscription Act of 1863. Yep, you could pay some poor sap a couple hundred dollars and he would go fight in your place. Cleveland decided he should stay at home and support his mother and sister while his two brothers were off fighting for the Union. His actions were made a part of his opponent's campaign during Cleveland's presidential race; but because it was legal, it had no impact on the voters.

What's the Flapper All About?

We've all heard glamorous stories of the Roaring Twenties, traditionally viewed as an era of great economic prosperity before the Great Crash of '29, when everyone was living high on the hog. But like many generalizations, it doesn't hold up under scrutiny. In fact, according to the Brookings Institution, although a handful of people did make fortunes, most people didn't get the lion's share of the Roaring Twenties. In 1929, 60 percent of American families had annual incomes of $2,000 or less (and 42 percent of these had annual incomes of less than $1,500). In 1929, families making less than $2,000 did not have enough money to meet the bare necessities of life—meaning nearly two-thirds of the population lived in poverty.

Stretching the Truth

Although lynching was popularized during the Old West, the practice actually started during the American Revolution. Colonel Charles Lynch, a justice of the peace and farmer before the war, led a group of vigilantes to dispense swift and final justice on British supporters and outlaws. Soon, stringing someone up without a trial became known as "lynching," and the groups that performed the activity were called "lynch mobs."

On Christmas Day in 1868, President Andrew Johnson's last significant act was granting unconditional amnesty to all Confederate soldiers for their actions in the Civil War. Confederate President Jefferson Davis declined to accept it.

His Final Bow

As one of his last official acts as president, Bill Clinton took it upon himself to take care of the number six man on the Department of Justice's list of "Most Wanted" international fugitives, Marc Rich. He gave him a full presidential pardon. But Rich wasn't the only beneficiary of Clinton's exit strategy: Carlos Anibal Vignali, who was serving fifteen years in prison for organized cocaine trafficking, got his prison sentence commuted, as did Almon Glenn Braswell, who had been convicted of mail fraud and perjury. In all, Clinton pardoned 140 people in the final days of his administration.

Hugh Rodham, brother of Hillary Rodham Clinton, lobbied the president for some of these pardons, receiving $400,000 in compensation. When ethical questions were raised (surprise), Rodham returned the money.

What Did You Call Me?

The Pilgrims who sailed on the *Mayflower* never referred to themselves as "Pilgrims." More than likely, they called themselves "Separatists" or even "Saints." The name "Pilgrim" was bestowed on them after the fact and was taken from William Bradford's journal (written between 1620 and 1647), *Of Plimoth Plantation* (in contemporary spelling, *Of Plymouth Plantation*). Bradford gave this name to his fellow travelers because a "pilgrim" is someone who takes a pilgrimage or an extensive journey to a holy location. Even though less than half of the 102 passengers on board the *Mayflower* were on a religious pilgrimage, Bradford referred to everyone on the voyage as pilgrims.

❧

In 1643, the colony of New Plymouth, Massachusetts, imposed the first recorded income tax in America.

A Flagging Interest

In paintings, movies, and on television, we're given the impression that worshipping the flag was something all devout Americans have done since the War of Independence, but that's not exactly the way it was. Schools were not required to fly the flag until 1890. Pledging allegiance to the flag wasn't instituted until 1892, and saluting the flag didn't happen until the time of the Spanish-American War in 1898. It wasn't until 1916 that Flag Day was observed as a national holiday, and the flag code, the proper way to treat and dispose of flags, was not approved by Congress until 1942 and didn't become a federal law until 1976.

And See Who Salutes It

So if Betsy Ross didn't design the first flag, who did? That person was probably Francis Hopkinson. On May 25, 1780, he wrote a letter to the Continental Board of Admiralty requesting a reward of "a Quarter Cask of the public Wine" for several patriotic designs he had created during the previous three years, including "the Flag of the United States of America." The request was sent to the Treasury Board, which turned it down in an October 27, 1780, report to Congress. The Board based their decision on the fact that Hopkinson "was not the only person consulted on those exhibitions of Fancy, and therefore cannot claim the sole merit of them and not entitled to the full sum charged."

Flag Runner Up

We know Betsy Ross was a poor, recently widowed, struggling seamstress who was secretly approached by General George Washington and two others, at a clandestine nighttime meeting. They begged for her help in creating the flag. So who is this Francis Hopkinson fellow trying to steal all the glory for creating Old Glory? Hopkinson was an American author, and, as a delegate from New Jersey, he was one of the signers of the Declaration of Independence.

In the Wrong Key

Some mistakenly believe that Francis Scott Key was an avid supporter of the War of 1812 and a known patriot—he was neither. Key was on board the British ship *HMS Tonnant* accompanied by American prisoner exchange agent Colonel John Stuart Skinner to negotiate the freeing of a political prisoner. In fact, Key was against the War of 1812, condemning "this abominable war" as a "lump of wickedness," and writing his mother that he thought the United States was the aggressor in the conflict and deserved defeat.

In 1861, Francis Scott Key's grandson was imprisoned in Fort McHenry (where Francis saw that "the flag was still there") along with the mayor of Baltimore and other locals deemed to be pro-South.

The Odd Couple

It's a romantic image to think of two of our founding fathers and best friends, Thomas Jefferson and John Adams, both dying on the Fourth of July in 1826 (exactly fifty years after the adoption of the Declaration of Independence). Each was thinking of the other just before he died. Adams is even supposed to have remarked just before he passed away, "Jefferson still survives." But were they friends? Well, just five years before their deaths, Adams accused Jefferson of plagiarizing the Declaration of Independence from the Mecklenburg Declaration, a document of North Carolina independence, which supposedly dated back to 1775. "Mr. Jefferson," Adams wrote a friend, "must have seen it, in the time of it, for he has copied the spirit, the sense, and the expressions of it verbatim, into his Declaration of the 4th of July, 1776." The authenticity of the Mecklenburg Declaration of Independence is still in question.

Raise Your Hand
if You're Not Sure

Between 1892 and 1942, Americans were taught to salute the flag with the so-called Bellamy salute (named after Francis Bellamy, 1855–1931, to accompany the Pledge of Allegiance, which he had written): The "right hand [is] lifted, palm downward, to a line with the forehead and close to it." But when the Nazis came into power, their salute and the American salute looked a little too similar for comfort. So, by order of Congress in 1942, Americans began "saluting" the flag by putting their right hand over their hearts.

"I pledge allegiance to the Flag of the United States of America and to the Republic for which it stands; one Nation, indivisible, with liberty and justice for all." President Dwight Eisenhower signed a bill into law on Flag Day (June 14, 1954) that added the words "under God" after "one Nation."

Ta-Da!

To commemorate the death of master magician Harry Houdini, Joseph W. "Amazing Joe" Burrus tried to better one of Houdini's famous stunts on October 31, 1990. Burrus was chained and locked, placed in a clear plastic coffin of his own making, and lowered into the ground. Then dirt and finally seven tons of concrete were poured on top of the coffin. Before Burrus could escape, the weight of the concrete crushed the coffin, and he died exactly sixty-four Halloweens from the day the Great Houdini died. J. D. Bristow, the stuntman's assistant on the fatal night, said Burrus made no attempt to calculate the weight of the dirt and concrete and tested the strength of the plastic coffin simply by jumping on it.

When the Civil War started, Union General Ulysses S. Grant owned slaves, but Confederate General Robert E. Lee did not.

A House Divided

Fighting in the Civil War wasn't all about glory, romanticism, unifying the country, or even freeing the slaves—it was also about money. More than 100,000 soldiers, mostly immigrants, were hired to fight for the North. However, if you were already rich and didn't need the money, or you didn't want to fight in the war, you could legally get out of the conscription by paying a $300 commutation fee. Some well-known people who paid their way out were banker J. P. Morgan and Theodore Roosevelt, Sr., father of President Theodore Roosevelt. But if paying wasn't an option, then you could do what more than 200,000 Union soldiers did after the war started—they deserted.

A Farewell to Arms

Ernest Hemingway has always been portrayed as a brave, hard-drinking, hard-living hunter, soldier, and writer—but he wasn't all those things. Hemingway did serve in World War I, but not as a soldier. He was a volunteer with the American Red Cross. He was wounded by mortar fire, but while serving chocolates to the soldiers. He was also in both the Spanish Civil War and World War II, but he served only as a reporter. Apparently, Hemingway's ability to weave a great story wasn't confined to the written page; he falsely claimed he was the first American wounded in Italy (after carrying an Italian soldier on his back to safety). He was never, as he claimed, wounded by machine-gun fire; he didn't join the Sixty-Ninth Infantry; and he never fought in three major Italian battles.

Horatio No You Didn't

The rags-to-riches stories of American author Horatio Alger are considered by many critics to be overly romantic and poorly written. Alger fans didn't care, because they bought his books by the millions, making him one of the best-selling authors of all times. But the chief complaint about Alger had nothing to do with his literary aptitude, but more with his morality. Alger, it turned out, was a notorious pedophile. According to Unitarian church records, in 1866, when Alger was a young pastor in Brewster, Massachusetts, several boys in his congregation accused him of using his position to take advantage of them sexually. Before he could be punished for his crimes, Alger left town and ended up in New York City, where he became known as a writer of children's fiction.

Just Squeaking By

Did Mickey Mouse make his debut in the animated short *Steamboat Willie*? Well, if he did, he wouldn't be in this book. Actually, Mickey first appeared in a silent film called *Plane Crazy*, but it was *Steamboat Willie* that was first shown in public. The movie made its debut at the Colony Theater in New York on November 18, 1928, and was the first cartoon that successfully incorporated synchronized sound. That is why November 18 is officially considered Mickey's birthday. But what do you get for a mouse that has everything?

We Deserve a Break Today

We've all heard the name Ray Kroc before—he's the guy who founded McDonald's. But if he was the founder, why didn't he call his franchise Kroc's, or even McKroc's? Obviously, no one would eat at a restaurant named McKroc's, but the real reason is that he wasn't the restaurant's founder. Richard and Maurice McDonald opened their first drive-in restaurant near Pasadena, California, and they started McDonald's in 1940. In 1954, Ray Kroc, who was a milkshake-machine salesman, bought the franchise rights from the brothers and eventually acquired the McDonald's name for $14 million. He completed his buyout in 1961. So, saying that Ray Kroc founded McDonald's is, well, a bunch of crock.

❧

Woodrow Wilson was the only president with a PhD.
He earned it from Johns Hopkins University in 1886.

What's Buggin' Ya?

In 1947, the U.S. Navy's Mark II computer at Harvard University crashed after a moth got jammed in a relay switch. The operators removed the fried flutter-by and taped it in their logbook alongside the explanation of the occurrence. It's a true story, but it doesn't describe the origin of the term "bug" (as in "computer bug"). A newspaper report from 1889, cited in the *Oxford English Dictionary*, related that Thomas Edison "had been up the two previous nights searching for a bug in his phonograph." And the 1934 edition of Webster's dictionary also gave the definition of bug as it related to a screw-up in a mechanical or electrical device.

Egg on His Face

In case you've ever wondered, Eggs Benedict is not named for the famous traitor Benedict Arnold. The origin of the name for the breakfast dish that consists of a half of an English muffin topped with ham or bacon, poached eggs, and hollandaise sauce is a mystery. Lemuel Benedict claimed he concocted the dish in 1894 at the Waldorf Hotel as a hangover remedy. Or maybe it was Commodore E. C. Benedict, or Mrs. Le Grand Benedict, or even the explanation given in the book *French Provincial Cooking*, which describes a traditional French dish named *œufs bénédictine*. However the name came about, it definitely has nothing to do with Benedict Arnold because if it was it would more than likely have been called Eggs Arnold.

Amending the Amendments

There's only been one time in our nation's history when one amendment to the Constitution was enacted to cancel out an earlier amendment. That took place in 1933 when the Twenty-First Amendment repealed the Eighteenth Amendment, which had prohibited the manufacture, sale, and transportation of liquor in the United States in 1919—basically, the Twenty-First Amendment prohibited Prohibition.

While a high school student in the early 1930s, Richard Nixon worked for two summers as a barker for the wheel-of-chance at the Slippery Gulch Rodeo in Prescott, Arizona.

Get This Party Started

The Republican party likes to refer to itself as the GOP or the Grand Old Party. But that isn't what GOP always stood for. The initials date back to the 1870s when they stood for "this gallant old party" in the 1875 Congressional Record. There is another reference in 1876 to "Grand Old Party," and "Get Out and Push" was used as a party slogan in the 1920s. But whether it's gallant or grand, it isn't the oldest party. The Democrat party organized in 1830 under Andrew Jackson actually is an off-shoot of the Democratic-Republicans from the era of Thomas Jefferson.

Never More

We all have the image of a stumbling Edgar Allan Poe, stoned out of his mind, passing out on a Baltimore sidewalk shortly before he died. We all know he was macabre, morbid, an alcoholic, and a dope fiend but still one of the greatest writers in American literature and the creator of the detective story. But most of the horrible attributes aren't true. An envious writer named Rufus Griswold, who wrote a biographical article of Poe called "Memoir of the Author," created them. Griswold wrote that Poe had "criminal relations with his Mother in Law," was a drunkard who was kicked out of both the University of Virginia and West Point, and was a depraved, drug-addled madman. Griswold used forged letters supposedly written by Poe to prove his case, and it was from this article that most people have garnered their information.

If You Lick It, It's a Quarter

The United States Post Office printed a new 60-cent stamp in 1999 that commemorated the Grand Canyon. It was a large, beautiful stamp that showed the canyon and bore the words "Grand Canyon, Colorado." The only problem is the Grand Canyon is in Arizona. Officials decided to destroy all 100 million stamps they had produced at a cost of about $500,000, and they reprinted the stamps with correct wording. The new and improved stamp went on sale in January 2000, but it was soon pointed out that the picture of the Grand Canyon was reversed, creating a mirror image of the canyon. The U.S.P.O. decided that since the stamps were already on sale, they would stick with the new stamp anyway.

Bully or Just Plain Bull?

The image of hundreds of men on horseback led by a barrel-chested Teddy Roosevelt, sword in hand, yelling "charge" as they conquered San Juan Hill and turned the tide of the Spanish-American War in favor of the Americans is an enduring image. It was that image that Teddy Roosevelt used in his charge into the White House, but it didn't happen. The "Rough Riders" charged Kettle Hill, not San Juan Hill, on foot because there wasn't enough room on board the ships for the men, their supplies, and their horses. So even though Roosevelt was famous for saying "bully"— he also said a lot of bull#$&t.

Colonel Leonard Wood, not Roosevelt, was actually in command of the charge on Kettle Hill. After the battle the "Rough Riders" renamed themselves "Wood's Weary Walkers."

What's in a Name?

Ulysses Simpson Grant was born in 1822 to Jesse and Hanna Grant. Actually, Jesse and Hanna Grant did have a baby boy but, when they finally named him a month later, they called him Hiram Ulysses Grant: Hiram for his grandfather and Ulysses for the Greek hero. When Hiram joined the U.S. Military Academy, his congressman incorrectly listed him as Ulysses Simpson Grant. Grant, who always disliked his name because his initials spelled H.U.G., decided to keep his newly appointed name. He never adopted it formally but used it as his own for the rest of his life.

The Slavery Bill

A lot of revisionists (people who want to rewrite history to make it politically correct) have torn into President Thomas Jefferson because he owned slaves. Some have even gone so far as to suggest removing his picture from the $2 bill (yes, there is a $2 bill). But if we're going to be consistent, we're going to be short a lot of money. There have been nine other presidents who also owned slaves: Washington (on the quarter and the $1 bill), Andrew Jackson ($20 bill), and Ulysses S. Grant ($50 bill). The other presidents—James Madison, James Monroe, John Tyler, James Knox Polk, Zachary Taylor, and Andrew Johnson—owned slaves, but they aren't on U.S. currency.

The Presidential Look

When Gerald Ford was chosen by Nixon to replace Spiro Agnew, many people wondered, "Who is this guy? What's he done before?" Well, among other things as a young man, Gerald Ford appeared in a 1939 edition of *Look* magazine with his girlfriend Phyllis Brown. It was an article about a weekend in the life of the "beautiful people." He later appeared on the cover of *Cosmopolitan*. Seems to make him as qualified to be president as nearly anyone else.

Grin and Bear it

At the Battle of Vicksburg during the Civil War, a servant girl accidentally poured out a basin containing Ulysses S. Grant's false teeth into the Mississippi River. He was unable to eat solid food for a week until a dentist came and made him a new set of choppers.

Julia Ward Howe (1819–1910) sold her poem, *Battle Hymn of the Republic*, which later was set to music, to the *Atlantic Monthly* in 1862 for $5.

Brand Names

Most people are stuck with the name they are given at birth unless they legally change it. However, in the history of the United States, there have been five presidents who altered their name—just a little. Grover Cleveland's real name was Stephen Grover Cleveland (which has a nice ring to it), but he decided to drop his first name, as did Thomas Woodrow Wilson and John Calvin Coolidge. Dwight David Eisenhower's real name was David Dwight Eisenhower; he didn't like the order and reversed his first and middle name.

There are four presidents who are known by their initials: Franklin Delano Roosevelt (FDR), John Fitzgerald Kennedy (JFK), Lyndon Baines Johnson (LBJ), and Theodore Roosevelt, who hated the nickname "Teddy" and preferred "TR" instead.

Johnny Rebel

John Tyler wasn't honored after his death on January 18, 1862, and no official word of his death was ever issued. Why? Because Tyler was considered a traitor in the North even though he had been president of the United States. On May 5, 1861, Tyler accepted a seat in the provisional congress of the Confederate States of America. A few months later, he was elected to represent his congressional district in the permanent C.S.A. Congress. Tyler was truly a rebel and the only president to ever hold office in the Confederacy. When he died, he even had the Confederate flag, not the American flag, draped over his casket. It wasn't until 1915, fifty years after the Civil War ended, that the United States finally erected a memorial stone over his grave.

The Good Ole Days— Part II

Here are more verbatim excerpts from the *Historical Summary of Conduct Cases in the House of Representatives* by the Committee on Standards of Official Conduct. Makes modern congressmen seem like pussycats.

- Representative William J. Graves (KY) and Representative Henry Wise (VA), Breach of the privileges of the House Representative Graves killed Representative Jonathan Cilley (ME) in a duel over words spoken in debate; Representative Wise acted as a second (Feb. 24, 1838).

- Representative Philemon Herbert (CA), (1856)
  Arrested for manslaughter (May 8, 1856); imprisoned prior to trial; acquitted (July 1856).

- Representative Lovell H. Rousseau (KY) (1866)
  Assaulted Representative Josiah Grinnell (IA) with a cane outside the Capitol for alleged insult spoken in debate (June 14, 1866).

But Do You Have a Record of It?

Thomas Edison worked on the ground floor of a telegraph company that used to be a restaurant and was literally crawling with cockroaches. The roaches, he said, would crawl out of the walls and up on his table while he was writing telegraphs. So he used his inventive mind and created a roach zapper. He placed a piece of tin foil on the ground and hooked it up to a "big battery supply current to the wires," so when the cockroach scampered across it "there was a flash of light and the cockroach went into gas."

Keep Your Trap Shut

Ralph Waldo Emerson was an American essayist, philosopher, and poet who is continuously quoted as saying that if you build a better mousetrap "The world will beat a path to your door." The genesis of that idea is contained in a journal entry written in 1855: "If a man can make better chairs or knives, crucibles or church organs, than anybody else, you will find a broad hard-beaten road to his house . . . " But nothing about mousetraps. Scholars have scoured Emerson's writings and have concluded that he never wrote anything about mousetraps. Apparently, Sarah Yule and Mary Keene, in a book published in 1889 (seven years after Emerson's death), decided that the list of things for which a man can earn public attention wouldn't be complete without a mousetrap, so they just threw that one in.

But Who's Counting?

When the Nineteenth Amendment to the Constitution was ratified on August 18, 1920, women were finally given the right to vote. Sounds pretty cut and dry, but of course, history is anything but cut and dry. During various times throughout American history, some women already had the right to vote, such as in local elections during colonial times in Massachusetts, New York, New Jersey, Rhode Island, and Pennsylvania. And between 1776 and 1807, women who were worth at least 50 pounds had the right to vote in New Jersey. In 1869, the Territory of Wyoming granted women voting rights in all elections, the Territory of Utah followed in 1870, and in 1883, so did the Territory of Washington. By the time the Nineteenth Amendment was ratified, women already had the vote in fifteen of the forty-eight states.

❧

While Martin Van Buren was vice president under
Andrew Jackson, he routinely presided over the
Senate wearing a pair of loaded pistols.

Run Out on a Rail

Abraham Lincoln's life is so steeped in myth, fiction, and legend that it's difficult to know what to believe. Like this oft-quoted pro-tariff statement attributed to him: "I do not know much about the tariff, but I know this much, when we buy manufactured goods abroad, we get the goods and the manufacturer gets the money. When we buy manufactured goods at home, we get both the goods and the money. When an American paid $20 for steel rails to an English manufacturer, America had the steel and England the $20. But when he paid $20 for the steel to an American manufacturer, America had both the steel and the $20." This one is easy to disprove. The reason Lincoln couldn't have said it was that he died before the first steel rails were brought into, or manufactured in, the United States.

Different Sides of the Same Coin

It is widely believed that most colonists wanted freedom from the tyranny of Great Britain and that there were few "loyalists," or people who remained loyal to the crown. That's simply not the case. In fact, there were a great number of loyalists who fought against the patriots. For example, in 1780 there were 9,000 patriots in Washington's army while 8,000 loyalists served in the British Army.

Always on the Winning Side

What is now Jackson, New Hampshire, was originally known as New Madbury, New Hampshire. The town changed its name in 1800 to Adams to honor the election of President John Adams. But in 1829, when John Adams's son John Quincy Adams lost the election to Andrew Jackson, the town changed its name to Jackson, New Hampshire.

In November 1939 during the Great Depression, Franklin D. Roosevelt ordered that Thanksgiving be celebrated one week earlier than usual, thereby extending the Christmas shopping season.

Stupid History

Keeping Up with the Joneses

Revolutionary hero John Paul Jones was actually born John Paul in 1747. He added the Jones part later. He is remembered for his bravery on the high seas and for supposedly remarking, "I've just begun to fight." But what isn't remembered about Jones is what he did after the Revolution. He left the United States, and in 1788 he became a well-paid mercenary in the service of Empress Catherine II of Russia. Once in her service, Jones once again took liberty with his name and changed from John Paul Jones to Pavel Dzhones.

A Jury of Your Peers

One would think that after women were given the right to vote in 1920, everything would be equal among the sexes. Far from it. As late as 1942, women only had the right to sit on a jury in twenty-eight states. It wasn't until 1957 that they were guaranteed the right to sit on federal juries. In 1973 they were finally given the right to sit on all juries in all fifty states.

When Jimmy Carter was the thirty-ninth president of the United States, he kissed England's queen mother, Queen Elizabeth, on the lips. It was a shocking breach of etiquette that even obituary writers noted upon her death.

Boston Beans

If there's one thing that makes Americans stiffen with pride and justification, it's the Boston Massacre. The idea of a group of fierce, armed British soldiers firing into a quivering, innocent group of patriots is beyond belief. And it should be, because it didn't happen the way we're led to believe. You see, it was the Americans who started the fight. The colonists were reacting to an incident earlier in the day. To protest the British presence in their town, a large angry mob estimated at between 300 and 400 people surrounded a small British garrison and threatened the troops with clubs and rocks. After Private Hugh Montgomery was struck with a club, he fired his weapon and other British soldiers followed suit. Five colonists were killed (three at the scene and two died later from their wounds), and six others were hurt.

B4 Boston

There were several less propagandized run-ins with the British before the Boston Massacre. A patriot in New York was wounded with a bayonet during a skirmish with British troops in 1766. Two years later, a Rhode Island man was killed in an argument with a British naval officer. And in New York in January 1770, there was a nasty battle between redcoats and patriots. The following month, during a patriot attack on the home of a Boston Tory, an eleven-year-old boy was killed.

Hell of a Party

Another great event in the history of the United States is the infamous Boston Tea Party. You know the story. On December 16, 1773, a group of colonists, angry at paying higher taxes on their tea, dressed up like Indians and dumped crates of tea bricks belonging to the British East India Company into the Boston Harbor. Not sure why we're so proud of an act of vandalism, but that's beside the point. The point is, the Tea Act, which the colonists were supposedly angry about, actually reduced the duty on British tea imported to America. So why did they really revolt? Because once British tea was affordable, it would ruin America's lucrative trade in black-market tea, because three-fourths of the tea sold in America was smuggled in by John Hancock. Now the whole idea of dressing up like Indians makes sense, doesn't it?

I Got No Strings to Hold Me Down

Richard Nixon resigned his presidency after it was uncovered that he had ordered the break-in of the Democratic election headquarters at the Watergate apartment complex in Washington, D.C. Years later, John Barrett, the first undercover officer to arrive on the scene, finally explained how the burglars had been apprehended. Apparently, the lookout stationed in the Howard Johnson Motel across the street did not see Barrett arrive because he was busy watching a movie on TV. The movie in question was the 1958 thriller *Attack of the Puppet People*.

The Watergate burglars used tape to hold down a door's spring-loaded lock mechanism so as not to be locked in. Their trick was noticed, however, because they applied the tape horizontally around the door rather than vertically along its edge.

And I'll Cry if I Want To

Although used as a catalyst to initiate the war for independence, not everyone agreed with the actions perpetrated during the Boston Tea Party. In fact, Benjamin Franklin suggested the colonists should reimburse the East India Company for the destroyed tea. A New York merchant, Robert Murray, and three others visited Lord North and offered to pay for the losses, but the offer was turned down.

A Real Sticky Situation

On an unusually warm January day in 1919, the fifty-foot-high tank at the Purity Distilling Company in Boston, Massachusetts, which contained more than 2 million gallons of steam-heated molasses, burst, sending a tidal wave of molasses into the streets. The wave, which reached fifteen feet, traveled at thirty-five miles an hour; it crushed trolley cars, swallowed trucks, horses, and carts, knocked buildings off their foundations, killed twenty-one people, and wounded 150 others. Finally, the molasses began to cool and congeal, and rescue teams arrived to help the survivors and find the victims. When the Red Cross workers arrived, they helped bandage the wounded and gave the survivors fresh hot coffee—sweetened with the molasses that still ran in the streets.

Forging Another Myth

Freezing, half-naked, half-starved soldiers leaving bloody footprints in the snow or shivering, huddled over a small fire—that's what most of us think of when we hear about Valley Forge during the winter of 1777–1778. But studies by the National Park Service showed that nobody starved or froze to death, and morale was high. The men usually had plenty to eat as the camp was supplied each month with a million pounds of flour and a million pounds of meat and fish. The men didn't live in the open but had constructed log houses that they described as "cozy and comfortable quarters." Not to say that there wasn't suffering or disease, but it wasn't the horrible situation we've been led to believe. And who led us to believe this way? General George Washington himself. Wanting to make sure his men had the supplies they needed, he resorted to stretching the truth a little about their situation.

The belief that some of the men went "naked" at Valley Forge results from misunderstanding the eighteenth-century use of the word. The term "naked" implied that the men did not wear proper clothing and were therefore considered unfit for duty, not that they had no clothes at all.

The Cane Mutiny

Charles Sumner, the Massachusetts senator who was clubbed over the head with a cane by a South Carolina representative, has become part of Civil War mythology. The event did happen, and it did follow Sumner's passionate speech on the "barbarism of slavery." But was the attack so severe that it left Sumner virtually incapacitated for three years? According to David Donald's Pulitzer prize–winning biography of Sumner, there is nothing in the senator's medical record to explain why he couldn't execute his duties. It's assumed that Sumner suffered more psychological than physical harm from the attack.

❧

"Elevate them guns a little lower!"

President Andrew Jackson, in 1815, at the battle of Mobile, Alabama

Afford the Truth

Henry Ford popularized both the automobile and the assembly line, but he was in no way responsible for their invention. The first automobile (non-gasoline powered) was the Puffing Devil, built and demonstrated by Richard Trevithick in 1801. Some suggest that Nicolas-Joseph Cugnot preceded Trevithick by more than thirty years, or even that Ferdinand Verbiest should be given credit for his steam-powered car built in 1672. However, there's no conclusive proof that either of these machines actually worked. The belief that Ford invented the moving assembly line is also an unwarranted claim. Ransom Olds (of Oldsmobile fame) patented the assembly line concept in 1901, and Ford implemented his assembly line in 1913.

Spirits of America

After retiring from the presidency on March 4, 1797, George Washington returned home to Mount Vernon and started a new career as a producer of whiskey. He constructed a 2,250 square foot distillery that housed five copper stills, a boiler, and fifty mash tubs. It became one of the largest distilleries in America at the time. Two years after its construction, the distillery produced 11,000 gallons of corn and rye whiskey and fruit brandy.

A Note to Congress

Thomas Jefferson only communicated with Congress through written messages, even though his predecessors addressed the legislature in person. Because of this practice, it wasn't until Woodrow Wilson that presidents began appearing in front of Congress personally. It is rumored that Jefferson wrote as opposed to speaking because he was a poor orator but an excellent writer.

If you think members of Congress are sneaky now (which you should because they are), look at the forty-second Congress of 1873. It not only gave itself a salary raise of 50 percent, but then made it retroactive for two years.

Home Sick

It's a type of rags to riches story, but it's more along the lines of a sick to healthy story. Theodore Roosevelt said that as a child, he was very sick and chronically asthmatic, but with fresh air and exercise, he became known as one of the most physically active presidents in history. However, in his biography of Roosevelt, David McCullough states that even though Roosevelt may have suffered as a child, he might not have been as sick as we've been led to believe. It seems that his asthma attacks occurred only on Sundays—the one day of the week that his father was at home.

Pulit Surprise

John F. Kennedy is the only president to date who has won the Pulitzer Prize. He was honored with the prestigious award in 1957 for his book *Profiles in Courage*. But like a lot of myths surrounding "Camelot," this one isn't quite true. Kennedy did win the Prize, but did he really write the book by himself? No. One of his speechwriters, Theodore Sorensen, actually penned most the book. This fact has been rumored for years, but it was Sorensen's own autobiography in 2008 that let the cat out of the bag. Sorensen wrote that he "did a first draft of most chapters," "helped choose the words of many of its sentences," and "privately boasted or indirectly hinted that [he] had written much of the book."

What's in a Dream

It's a chilling story and another fascinating aspect of the life of President Abraham Lincoln—that he had a premonition of his own death by an assassin's bullet. Several days before his death, Lincoln told of a dream in which he had been awakened in the White House by mournful cries and discovered that the wailing voices were coming from the East Room. "There I met with a sickening surprise. Before me was a catafalque, on which rested a corpse wrapped in funeral vestments. 'Who is dead in the White House?' I demanded of one of the soldiers. 'The President' was his answer; 'he was killed by an assassin.'" So Lincoln *did* predict his own death! No, because when the story was originally published, Lincoln made it clear that it wasn't he who had been killed. "In this dream," the president was quoted as saying, "it was not me, but some other fellow, that was killed. It seems that this ghostly assassin tried his hand on someone else."

Not Very Revered

In July 1779, forty-five American ships sailed into Penobscot Bay where the British held a half-finished fort, but the Americans did nothing to provoke the enemy. Even though they outnumbered the British, they waited for weeks without taking any action, and that gave the British plenty of time to bring in reinforcements. Confronted by a well-manned army and navy, the American ships fled up the Penobscot River. Realizing they might be attacked by the British and have their supplies and ships captured, they decided to burn seventeen of their own ships and fled by foot. Paul Revere (yes, that Paul Revere), who was the commander of artillery, was charged by the Continental Army with cowardice and insubordination. (One military committee ruled that Revere's conduct was "crityzable"; another that it was not.) However, Revere was acquitted during his court martial in 1782.

Any Last Words?

An interesting story about Benedict Arnold, and one that shows he repented his treason, is that on his death bed he cried out, "Let me die in my American uniform in which I fought my battles. God forgive me for ever putting on any other." It's a great redemptive story, but it isn't true. After his death, Arnold's wife Margaret "Peggy" Shippen Arnold wrote that Benedict had been delirious in his last three days and wasn't able to swallow or speak a word.

***

When John F. Kennedy was assassinated in
Dallas in 1963, it was not a federal felony to kill
a president of the United States.

The Final Act

Pulitzer Prize– and Tony Award–winning playwright Tennessee Williams, famous for *A Streetcar Named Desire* and *Cat on a Hot Tin Roof,* suffocated to death at the age of seventy-one on February 24, 1983, in his room at the Hotel Elysee in New York City. Coroners discovered that Williams had choked to death on an eye-drop bottle cap, which friends said he would routinely place in his mouth when he tilted back his head to administer the eye drops.

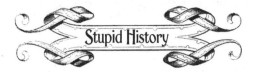

The Woodstock Festival, technically called The Woodstock Music and Art Fair, was actually held at Max Yasgur's dairy farm in the rural town of Bethel, New York, forty-three miles southwest of Woodstock, New York.

English First

Martin Van Buren, the first president born an American citizen (his predecessors were born before the War of Independence) grew up speaking Dutch, which made him the only president not to have spoken English as a first language (unless, of course, you include George W. Bush).

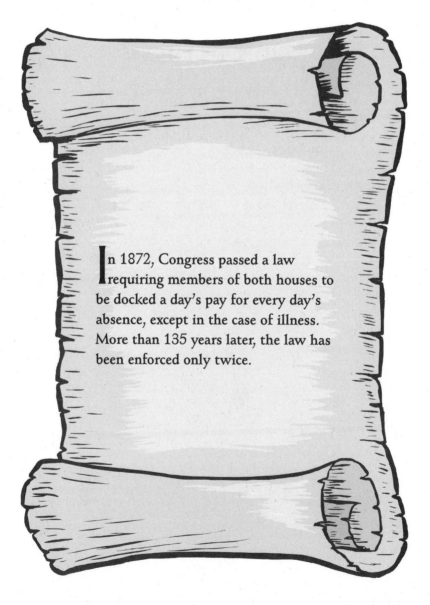

In 1872, Congress passed a law requiring members of both houses to be docked a day's pay for every day's absence, except in the case of illness. More than 135 years later, the law has been enforced only twice.

The Shot Heard Around the World

In a horrible perversion on the old saying, "third time's a charm," John Wilkes Booth was actually the third assassin who attempted to take the life of President Abraham Lincoln. Lincoln had been the target of two failed assassination attempts, both times while on his way to his cottage at the Soldiers' Home on the outskirts of Washington, D.C. In his book *Abraham Lincoln*, Carl Sandburg tells of the first attempt in 1861, when Lincoln was shot at by a man standing less than fifty yards away. Then in August 1864, he was shot at again, and this time the bullet passed through the upper part of his famous stovepipe hat. But it was that third, fatal bullet we all remember, fired at pointblank range on April 14, 1865.

What's Burnin' Ya?

The War of 1812 is remembered (if at all) for one thing—the burning of the White House by those dastardly British. Invading a country is one thing, but to maliciously burn down important and cherished buildings is just mean. But that's just what *we* did to the British before they did it to us. The Americans attacked York, the capital of Upper Canada (which became Toronto, Ontario), on April 27, 1813, and burned dozens of buildings including the Parliament, all without orders. Because of this malicious attack, the British retaliated with their burning of Washington, D.C. on August 24, 1814.

Take a Letter

On November 21, 1864, the *Boston Evening Transcript* printed a letter from President Abraham Lincoln to Mrs. Lydia Bixby, a widow who was "the mother of five sons who have died gloriously on the field of battle." The letter, known as the Bixby Letter, was both heartfelt and beautifully written, but there are two things wrong with it. One, it probably wasn't written by Abraham Lincoln (Lincoln's secretary John Hay later claimed to have penned the letter), and two, Mrs. Bixby's sons weren't all killed. According to War Department statistics, only two of Bixby's sons died (Charles and Oliver), one deserted, another was honorably discharged, and one was captured and became a Confederate (or died a POW). The original letter doesn't exist as Mrs. Bixby, who was a Confederate sympathizer and disliked President Lincoln, destroyed it shortly after it was delivered.

Soldiers of Misfortune

It was the most notorious military prison during the Civil War—Camp Sumter, commonly referred to as Andersonville Prison, located in Andersonville, Georgia. Of the 45,000 Union prisoners held there 12,913 died of malnutrition and disease—approximately 100 prisoners died every day. But it wasn't out of cruelty that the soldiers suffered so during their imprisonment, it was primarily because of overcrowding and the fact that the South couldn't afford to feed, clothe, or provide proper medical treatment for the prisoners. Other military prisons didn't fare much better. In fact, of the 195,000 Union soldiers imprisoned in the South, 15.5 percent died; and of the 215,000 Confederates imprisoned in the North, 12 percent died.

The commandant at Camp Sumter, Henry Wirz, was court-martialed, found guilty of war crimes, and hanged on November 10, 1865. Wirz was the only Confederate official to be tried and convicted of war crimes resulting from the Civil War.

Short and Stout

As ten-year-old Henry Ford watched steam rising from his mother's teapot, he deduced that if the steam were confined, it could raise the teapot into the air. He took a clay teapot, filled it with water, corked the spout, tied down the lid and placed the teapot in the fireplace. He watched the teapot carefully for signs that it was about to lift off, but what it did was blast off, or actually, blast apart. The exploding teapot broke a window and a mirror, scalded and cut young Henry, and left a scar on his face that he carried with him for the rest of his life.

❧

During the 1918 influenza pandemic, the death toll
in the United States was so high there was a shortage of coffins.

Dude Looks Like a Lady

A story told by Civil War buffs about Confederate president Jefferson Davis was that he had disguised himself in his wife's clothing when he was arrested on May 10, 1865. The event was widely publicized, and articles and cartoons portrayed Jefferson as a humiliated, cross-dressing coward. But, like many Civil War myths, it's not true. "I was in the party that captured Davis," Captain James H. Parker wrote later. "Jefferson Davis did not have on, at the time he was taken, any garments such as are worn by women."

Loose Lips

The unprovoked sinking of the *Lusitania* is regarded by many as the inciting incident that brought the United States into World War I. Although the sinking incident did heighten anti-German sentiment, it didn't bring the Americans into the war. Here are the facts: First, the ship was British, not American, even though 128 of the 1,198 killed were Americans; second, the Germans warned in advance that they would torpedo ships on the open seas; third, the *Lusitania* was carrying small arms ammunition (so it wasn't a neutral ship); and finally, the ship was sunk on May 7, 1915, and the Americans didn't declare war on Germany until April 6, 1917 (nearly two years later).

Run Away!

On June 4, 1754, a twenty-one-year-old lieutenant colonel in the Virginia militia and his men were ordered to build a fort and confront the French forces near what is now Pittsburgh. When they got to the location, they discovered the French had already occupied a fort called Duquesne. So the young officer attacked a French work party, took some prisoners, and then hurriedly constructed the aptly named Fort Necessity. The French immediately attacked, surrounded the newly constructed fort, and sent the lieutenant colonel and his men back to Virginia where, oddly enough, he was hailed as a hero. Unwittingly, the young Lieutenant Colonel George Washington had ordered the shots that began the French and Indian War.

What's Your Sign?

Benjamin Franklin was the only person to put his signature on all four primary documents that created the United States of America: the Treaty of Peace with Great Britain, the Declaration of Independence, the Treaty of Alliance with France, and the Constitution of the United States.

Run, Jesse, Run

After Jesse Owens won a gold medal in the 1936 Olympics in Berlin, Germany, Adolf Hitler refused to shake his hand because he was black. This would certainly fit the impression we have of Hitler, but the story just isn't true. It's true that Hitler didn't congratulate Owens, but he didn't congratulate any of the winners, even citizens of his own country, after the first day of the Olympics. That's because he was abiding by the International Olympic Committee's recommendation that he remain neutral. Owens even stood up for Hitler when he said, "Hitler didn't snub me—it was FDR who snubbed me. The president didn't even send me a telegram." Owens recalled that he had received the greatest ovations of his career in the Olympic Stadium in Berlin.

Not Like the West

The popular image of the early history of the Old West as a rough-and-tumble, shoot 'em up, violent, gun-fighting, homicidal era in American history is highly overrated—or, in other words, not really true. The main perpetrators of this image are the pulp fiction writers and, of course, Hollywood. In fact, more people die in most individual Hollywood westerns than died in an entire year in the West's toughest towns. In 1878, the most violent year in Dodge City, only five people were killed. In the South Dakota town of Deadwood, only four people were killed in its most homicidal year. And in Tombstone, Arizona, the infamous hometown of the shoot-out at the OK Corral in 1881, only five people were killed (three during the shoot-out).

Not All Black and White

If a question on a history test asked whether it was the North or the South that first forbade slavery, most people would answer the North. Surprisingly, that event first took place in the South—the deep South, in fact—in Georgia. In 1735, three years after Georgia was founded, its trustees outlawed the importation of blacks to the colony to forestall slavery. A short fifteen years later, under tremendous pressure from big planters, the trustees reversed their decision and allowed blacks to be brought into the colony as slaves.

Gerald Ford was sworn in as president a short
twenty-eight minutes after the secretary of state
received Richard Nixon's letter of resignation.

A Wing and a Prayer

Here's another George Washington myth that has burrowed its way into our national consciousness: the image of General Washington kneeling in the snow at Valley Forge deep in prayer. The story came from Mason Locke Weems (generally referred to as Parson Weems), the same man who created the "Washington chopped down the cherry tree" myth. In 1918, the Valley Forge Park Commission issued a report stating, "In none of these [documents] were found a single paragraph that will substantiate the tradition of the 'Prayer at Valley Forge.'" But still the image lives on.

Photos Don't Lie

Another endearing American image (and one used in dozens of history books) is Thomas Hill's rendition of the golden spike ceremony. The ceremony was in celebration of the First Transcontinental Railroad, connecting the Union Pacific and Central Pacific railroads, on May 10, 1869, at Promontory Summit, Utah. Hill's painting shows women in formal, elegant dresses, and men in fancy frock coats standing in front of several beautiful fluttering American flags. The actual photograph of the event shows something entirely different: Most of the men were wearing work clothes, several holding liquor bottles and looking intoxicated, and there were also a few sleazy-looking camp prostitutes.

No Place Like Home

The myths surrounding the Pilgrims are so numerous that one even involves what type of housing they lived in. Many Americans believe, usually because of artists' paintings, that the Pilgrims lived in log cabins. They didn't. The Pilgrims were English so they brought with them traditional English building construction methods, and that certainly wouldn't have been log cabins. The Germans and the Swedes introduced log cabins nearly a century later, and there's no record of the term "log cabin" being used before the 1770s. Although we have no definitive proof of what a Pilgrim house looked like, it would probably have been a simple frame structure (due to the plentiful amount of wood). We do know that by late 1621 they had constructed seven dwellings for communal living, including four storehouses, and two years later they had twenty houses standing.

The Real Casey Jones

Casey Jones is the legendary railroad folk hero—the man who sacrificed his life to save the lives of the passengers on his train. He *is* legendary, and he *is* a hero—because he was a real person and not a myth. John Luther "Casey" Jones (1863–1900) was an American railroad engineer from Jackson, Tennessee, who worked for the Illinois Central Railroad. On April 30, 1900, his fireman Sim Webb was shoveling coal when he saw the signal flags and red lights of a stopped freight train on the same track ahead of them. Jones told Webb to jump, which he did, and by staying at the controls and bringing the speed of his train down from seventy-five to thirty-five miles an hour, he saved the lives of the passengers on his train. Jones was the only person to die in the wreck, and he was immortalized for his courage in a popular ballad sung by his friend Wallace Saunders.

Don't Have a Cow, Man II

Many of us are familiar with the story of Mrs. O'Leary's cow kicking over a lantern and starting the Great Chicago Fire of 1871, and much of it is true. The fire did start in Catherine O'Leary's barn house at 137 DeKoven Street, and she did have a cow. But whether the cow was the true culprit is the center of the controversial myth. The fire probably started while her son James and two of his friends, Daniel "Pegleg" Sullivan and Louis M. Cohn, were gambling in the barn. When Mrs. O'Leary came out around 9 p.m. to chase them away, the lantern got knocked over by mistake. Michael Ahern, a *Chicago Tribune* reporter, admitted several years after the fire that he had made up the story of the cow kicking over the lantern because it was more interesting copy.

❧

The site of Mrs. O'Leary's barn now houses the Chicago Fire Department training school.

Pumping Irony

It may sound like a tragically ironic myth that on the night the *Titanic* sank they were showing the film *The Poseidon Adventure*, about a group of people trying to stay alive after their ocean liner capsized. But it's true. Two films were scheduled during the voyage and both had nautical themes: The 1911 movie *The Lighthouse Keeper* starring Mary Pickford played on the evenings of April 12 and 13, and *The Poseidon Adventure*, directed by D. W. Griffith, played on April 14. The movie began at 11 p.m. and people were so enthralled by the action, they didn't notice their ship jolting when it hit the fatal iceberg forty minutes later.

One Hump or Two?

In 1856, Secretary of War Jefferson Davis (who several years later would become the president of the Confederate States of America) ordered seventy camels brought to the United States from the Middle East. Davis realized that camels would be much better suited for travels across desert regions, didn't need much water, could eat desert vegetation, and could carry more than even the largest horse or mule could carry. The U.S. Camel Corps was established at Camp Verde, Texas, in the hill country north of San Antonio. But the camels didn't work out as expected; they were very stubborn, required special handlers, and scared the horses. In less than two years, the entire Corps was dismantled and a number of the camels were set loose in the desert.

In the mid-1870s, one of the abandoned camels wandered into Fort Selden, New Mexico, territory. The strange beast terrified the post commander's young son, who ran to hide behind his mother. The commander was Captain Arthur MacArthur, whose son grew up to be General of the Army Douglas MacArthur.

Don't Earn an "A"

The Puritans in Salem, Massachusetts, passed a law in 1695 that imposed severe punishment on a person convicted of the crime of adultery. First, the perpetrator would have to wear the letter "A" on a conspicuous part of his or her clothes for the rest of their lives (which inspired Nathaniel Hawthorne's story *The Scarlet Letter*).

An adulterer could also receive forty lashes from a whip and be required to sit on the gallows, with chains around the neck, for at least one hour. However, in the seventeenth century the penalty for adultery in Massachusetts was death. Even with this form of punishment looming over their heads, when the population of Boston hovered around 4,000 people, there were still forty-eight children born out of wedlock and fifty instances of fornication.

Two-Timing, Two-Year President

During his short two-year term, the twenty-ninth president of the United States, Warren Harding, was known for only a few things: having a corrupt administration, gambling, and womanizing. Before he became president, he had an affair with a woman named Carrie Phillips who demanded marriage although she was still married to someone else at the time. She had all of Harding's love letters and threatened to blackmail him even though he had already given her a Cadillac and promised her $5,000 a year. His campaign manager, Albert Lasker, bought her vow of silence with an all-expense-paid trip around the world (with her husband) under the condition that they depart before the election and not return until after.

Harding also had an affair with a woman named Nan Britton, with whom he was cheating on both his wife, Florence, and his mistress, Carrie Phillips. Britton was a virgin when they first met, and they continued their relationship while Harding was in office. It was known that when Nan visited the White House, they would sneak off and have sex in a small five-by-five-foot coat closet.

I'll Grant You That

There have been a few notorious presidential siblings, such as
Billy Carter, Roger Clinton, Sam Houston Johnson, and "Big
Don" Nixon, but none of them hold a candle to the likes of Ulysses
S. Grant's younger brother, Orvil. Orvil and Grant's secretary of war,
William Belknap, hit upon the idea of demanding kickbacks from the
franchising of highly profitable trading posts on the western front. Because
of regulations, soldiers were forced to exclusively use army trading posts
to make purchases. The money demanded by Grant and Belknap forced
the trading post owners to jack up their prices so high that General George
Armstrong Custer complained. Custer even testified against Belknap and
implicated Orvil Grant during a Senate investigation—another reason why
the administration of Ulysses S. Grant is considered the most scandal-ridden
of all presidencies.

Go with the Flow

Would you believe that an earthquake once reversed the course of the Mississippi River? The truth is, it wasn't one earthquake but three in 1811 and 1812 that changed the river's course. The New Madrid Fault Zone, which lies between Memphis and St. Louis, experienced three earthquakes registering approximately 8 on the Richter scale. They sent shockwaves along the Mississippi and altered the river's flow.

✦

Franklin D. Roosevelt served a record 4,422 days as president of the United States.

Nearly a Dual Duel

On July 11, 1804, Vice President Aaron Burr killed Alexander Hamilton during a duel. In 1797, Hamilton had nearly dueled with future president James Monroe, and it was Aaron Burr who stepped in and stopped the confrontation. After his duel with Hamilton, Burr was charged with murder in both New York and New Jersey, but neither case ever went to trial. To let the smoke settle, Burr fled to South Carolina but soon returned to Washington, D.C., and finished out his term as vice president.

Shut Your Mouth!

For reasons still unknown, Texas Congressman Thomas Lindsay Blanton, a Presbyterian Sunday-school teacher and prohibitionist, inserted dirty words into the *Congressional Record* in 1921. His colleagues overwhelmingly censured him on October 24, 1921, by a vote of 293–0.

❧

The first motto that appeared on U.S. coins was not "In God We Trust"; it was "Mind Your Business." These copper cents were authorized on April 21, 1787.

A Real Six-Shooter

Political duels usually leave one person dead or wounded, but rarely do they cause laughter. One exception was the case of the 1836 duel between two congressmen, Jesse Bynum of North Carolina and Daniel Jenifer of Maryland. Bynum loudly objected to Jenifer's denouncement of the course of President Jackson's party, and after a brief shouting match they were off to a shooting match. Both men arrived at the Bladensburg Dueling Ground, paced off ten feet, and fired. No one was hit. So they reloaded and shot again. Again, they both missed. The same result happened on the third, fourth, and fifth shots. As they prepared for the sixth round, Bynum's pistol accidentally discharged. One of Jenifer's seconds leveled his pistol at Bynum, but Jenifer ordered him to halt. Then Jenifer aimed carefully at Bynum, pulled the trigger—and missed. The duel was called off, and the two dishonored men agreed to a draw.

He Was Pasty White

It was one of the most reported political sex scandals of the 1970s—the story of Arkansas Representative Wilbur Mills and notorious stripper Fanne Foxe. U.S. Park Police stopped Mills, chairman of the powerful House Ways and Means Committee, in the early morning hours of October 7, 1974, for speeding with his lights off. Mills had four companions in the car and one of them, Fanne Foxe, stepped out and jumped into the murky waters of Washington's Tidal Basin. Mills, who was intoxicated, had a bloody nose and several scratches on his face that he claimed were the result of trying to restrain Foxe. But a little scandal between the most powerful man in Congress and a stripper wasn't enough to bother the good people of Arkansas, who re-elected Mills to another term.

The Real Fall Guy

It's an event in American history that is frequently referenced when discussions of political corruption surface: the Teapot Dome Scandal. But what exactly was it, and what's with the weird name? In 1922, the U.S. secretary of the interior under Warren Harding, Albert B. Fall, leased the Teapot Dome oil reserves (so named because of the site's resemblance to a giant sandstone teapot) without competitive bidding. He also leased other oil fields in exchange for "loans" amounting to $400,000 from Harry Sinclair and E. L. Doheny, multimillionaire oil producers doing business as Mammoth Oil Company and Pan-American Petroleum and Transport Company, respectively. What makes the scandal historical, apart from its catchy name, is that Fall became the first cabinet member in history to serve time in prison.

Say It Ain't So, Joe

Wisconsin Senator Joe McCarthy, notorious for the communist witch-hunts of the 1950s, was first elected after campaigning on a much-touted record of military service during World War II, christening himself "Tail-Gunner Joe." But McCarthy never actually served as a tail-gunner—he flew as a gunner-observer. He later claimed to have flown thirty-two missions when, in fact, he had only flown twelve.

Sickles in a Pickle

Congressman Dan Sickles is known for a number of things: as a Union general in the Civil War, as a U.S. minister to Spain, for being censured by the New York State Assembly for escorting known prostitute Fanny White into its chambers, and for being the first man in U.S. history to use temporary insanity as a legal defense. In 1859, Sickles was accused of murdering his wife's paramour, Philip Barton Key, son of Francis Scott Key. And although he confessed to the murder, his lawyer claimed he had been driven temporarily insane by his wife's infidelity. The public loved him (because he was protecting other innocent women from the evil lustfulness of Key), and apparently, the jury bought it: Sickles was acquitted.

Sickles went on to win the Congressional Medal of Honor for his acts of bravery during the Civil War and for the fact that he got one of his legs blown off during the Battle of Gettysburg.

The Bunny Hop

Collectors love to acquire the first edition of their favorite magazines. But if you're looking for the first issue of *Playboy* dated December 1, 1953—you're out of luck. There is no such issue. When Hugh Hefner published the first issue of *Playboy* he didn't know if there would be a second and, therefore, decided not to date it. Interestingly enough, *Playboy* was first titled *Stag Party*, but the publisher of a hunting magazine called *Stag* forced Hefner to rename his girly magazine.

The story that Hugh Hefner took the nude photograph of his first centerfold, Marilyn Monroe, on rumpled red velvet, is an urban legend. Photographer Tom Kelly made the now infamous photograph in 1949, and it had already appeared in calendars before Hefner paid $500 for the rights to use it in his magazine.

A Mickey Mouse Operation

One of the most underreported protests of the early 1970s was the Yippies' invasion of Disneyland on August 6, 1970. Hundreds of long-haired youths reacted to leaflets and advertisements placed in the *Los Angeles Free Press* inviting "Yippies" to attend the First International "Yippie Pow Wow" at Disneyland—lovingly called "Yippie Day." The Yippies were encouraged to attend this non-sponsored event "to liberate Minnie Mouse, have free rein of the park and infiltrate Tom Sawyer's Island." The other causes listed were for a Women's Lib rally to free Tinkerbell and a Black Panther hot breakfast at Aunt Jemima's. Disneyland decided to close early even though there was no violence, and most of the Yippies simply acted Goofy.

I Object!

Highly acclaimed marksman and World War I hero Alvin Cullum York (1887–1964) from Pall Mall, Tennessee, earned the Medal of Honor for capturing, along with seven other men, 132 Germans during the Meuse-Argonne Offensive in France. "Sergeant York," as he will forever be known, although he was only a corporal at the time, did capture a German machine gun nest on October 8, 1918, killing twenty-eight Germans, capturing thirty-two machine guns, and taking 132 Germans prisoner. But before he became a hero, York, a deeply religious man, had applied to be a conscientious objector to the war. However, because his religion (Church of Christ in Christian Union) wasn't recognized as a church at the time, he was drafted into the Army.

Oh, Say Can You See?

We've all heard the story of how Francis Scott Key, watching the bombardment of Fort McHenry during the Battle of Baltimore on the night of September 13, 1814, was so awestruck that he wrote a little poem that turned into the national anthem of the United States, *The Star Spangled Banner*. Key was approximately eight miles away during the attack and couldn't have possibly seen the normal "storm flag," a small flag designed expressly for bad weather, which flew during the battle and the night. According to the eyewitness testimony of Midshipman Robert J. Barrettas, as the British fleet sailed away the next morning, the Americans "hoisted a most superb and splendid ensign on their battery." This flag, which is on display at the Smithsonian in Washington, D.C., is enormous: thirty feet by forty-two feet. So what Keys saw "so gallantly streaming" was the newly hoisted flag—not the flag that flew during the battle.

Dumb Ass

How did the Democrats become known as the party of the donkey? It all started when Andrew Jackson ran for president in 1828 with the slogan, "Let the people rule," and his opponents tried to label him a "jackass." Jackson, however, turned the tables on his "neigh"-sayers by using the donkey, representing his stubbornness, on his campaign posters.

The Donkey symbol of the Democrat party was first used in a political cartoon in 1837 titled "A Modern Baalim and his Ass." Again the symbol was used in conjunction with Andrew Jackson. Even though he had left office by this time, he still thought of himself as the party's leader. He was shown in the cartoon trying to push the donkey where he wanted it to go.

Child's Play

Samuel Slater (1768–1835) was popularly known as the "Founder of the American Industrial Revolution," but he was also the founder of something else—the use of child labor. Slater's mill opened in Pawtucket, Rhode Island, in 1793 and started with nine workers, all of them children under the age of twelve. By 1830, 55 percent of the mill workers in Rhode Island were children.

❧

During the Civil War and especially in military prisons, illness and disease were so common that twice as many soldiers died of sickness as died in battle.

Supply and Demand

The term GI is used to describe members of the United States armed forces or equipment issued by the U.S. government. It is widely believed that the term GI therefore stands for "Government Issue" or "General Issue" or even "General Infantry." But on supply records, the initials originally preceded any equipment made from galvanized iron, such as trashcans. American soldiers during World War I commonly referred to incoming German artillery shells as "GI cans." The term slowly morphed, and by World War II it meant anything issued by the government— including soldiers.

❧

After leaving office, President Calvin "Silent Cal"
Coolidge went on to write a nationally syndicated newspaper
column, "Calvin Coolidge Says," from 1930 to 1931.

The Eagle Has Landed

It has been rumored that the Seal of the President of the United States, which shows an eagle holding an olive branch in its left talon and arrows in the other, is modified so that the eagle's head is turned to signify whether we're at war or peace. But it's not true. According to Bill Allman, White House curator, there is just one Seal of the President and the head faces toward the olive branch. This rumor might have started because before 1945, the eagle's head did face the arrows. President Harry Truman had it modified after World War II.

By Any Means Necessary

President Lyndon Johnson needed a reason to launch a full-scale invasion of Vietnam but couldn't justify it to the American people—until three North Vietnamese patrol ships fired on an American ship keeping watch on the Tonkin Gulf. Two days later, there was a report that a second attack on American ships was under way, and the president pleaded with Congress for action. This second attack provoked Congress to pass the Gulf of Tonkin Resolution on August 10, 1964, giving Johnson authorization, without a formal declaration of war by Congress, to use military force in Southeast Asia. But the second attack never happened, and it was known that it hadn't happened by Johnson's administration. But it's what they needed to ramp up what would become known as the Vietnam War.

The Gulf of Tonkin Resolution unanimously passed the House with only forty minutes of debate. Congress wasn't aware that the resolution had been drafted several months before the Gulf of Tonkin Incident ever took place.

A Wake-Up Call

During the days of the Pilgrims, church services weren't confined to today's standard one-hour sermon. In fact, they would routinely go on for up to seven hours. So how did the Pilgrims keep people awake that long? A simple device, which consisted of a wooden ball on the end of a length of string, served to bonk the nodding member of the congregation awake.

Ironically, the Constitution of the Confederate States of America forbade the practice of importing slaves from outside the Confederacy.

Look It Up

Infamous American dictionary maker Noah Webster adamantly hated the British and was simultaneously filled with American pride. He thought total separation from the English and their language was in order. "America must be as independent in literature as she is in politics," he wrote, and for him that included freedom from British spelling. Webster published his first dictionary, *A Compendious Dictionary of the English Language*, in 1806, and included his Americanized spellings. "Centre" was changed to "center," "honour" to "honor," and "programme" to "program." "Colour" became "color," "theatre" changed to "theater," "travelling" to "traveling," and so on. But his attempt to change "tongue" to "tung" didn't meet with much success.

Spare the Rod

Connecticut laws in the late 1600s were, to say the least, strict. Here is one example:

> "If any man have a stubborn or rebellious Son, of sufficient understanding and years, viz. fifteen years of age, which will not obey the voice of his Father, or the voice of his Mother, and that when they have chastened him, he will not hearken unto them; then may his Father or Mother, being his natural Parents, lay hold on him, and bring him to the Magistrates assembled in Court, and testified unto them, that their Son is Stubborn and Rebellious, and will not obey their voice and chastisement, but lives in sundry notorious Crimes, such a Son shall be put to death, Deut. 21:20–21."

The Deut. 21:20–21 reference denotes that the city elders got this law from that particular passage from Deuteronomy in the Bible.

Doubting Thomas

In 1801, Vice President Thomas Jefferson presented to Congress his *Manual of Parliamentary Practice*, in part because of the occasional tantrums that erupted in the Senate. One telling passage reads as if it had been written by a teacher of an unruly classroom: "No one is to disturb another in his speech by hissing, coughing, spitting, speaking or whispering to another; nor to stand up or interrupt him; nor to pass between the Speaker and the speaking member; nor to go across the [Senate chamber], or to walk up and down it, or to take books or papers from the [clerk's] table, or write there."

Still Seems Like a Good Idea

On April 27, 1911, Congressman Victor Berger of Wisconsin introduced a constitutional amendment to the House of Representatives that would abolish . . . the Senate. The preamble to the amendment read, "Whereas the Senate in particular has become an obstructive and useless body, a menace to the liberties of the people, and an obstacle to social growth." A Congressional committee quickly and quietly squashed the amendment.

Not with a Bang

The Civil War got its start during the Battle of Fort Sumter in Charleston Harbor, South Carolina, on April 12, 1861. One would think that a battle that kicked off such a war would have been bloody with a high body count, but it wasn't. In fact, no one died during the one-day battle. There was a casualty, however, when Private Daniel Hough was killed when the cannon he was loading accidentally discharged. That incident happened on April 14, the day after the battle ended, during a surrender ceremony.

The Chosen People

It was called General Order No. 11, and it was the instructions for the expulsion of all Jews in particular military districts during a war—but it wasn't World War II and the person who issued the order wasn't Hitler. It was Major General Ulysses S. Grant and the order was issued on December 17, 1862, during the American Civil War. Grant was convinced that "mostly Jews and other unprincipled traders" were controlling the black-market trade in Southern cotton in Tennessee, Mississippi, and Kentucky. President Abraham Lincoln revoked the order a few weeks later following an outcry of protest from Jewish community leaders and members of both the press and Congress. Grant later shifted the blame to a subordinate, claiming he had written the order and Grant had just added his signature without reading the document.

Stone Cold Stonewall

During the Battle of Chancellorsville, Virginia, from April 30 to May 6, 1863, Confederate General Thomas "Stonewall" Jackson gave strict orders to shoot any unknown or unidentified solider who approached their lines and to ask questions later. And, you guessed it, when Jackson and some of his men were returning from a reconnaissance mission, they were fired upon by their own troops. Jackson was wounded in his left arm; eight days later it was amputated. Following complications from pneumonia, Jackson died. He was considered by many to be the best strategist in the Confederate Army and quite possibly of either side.

You Can Ring My Bell

The story of the Liberty Bell as we know it today came from an 1847 book entitled *Washington and His Generals: or, Legends of the American Revolution* by George Lippard, a Philadelphia journalist. Lippard was the one who created the whole story of the bell's involvement in American independence, and thus he forged forever one of the greatest mythical symbols of American freedom.

President Lincoln had four brothers-in-law
who fought for the Confederacy.

Ice Capades

The theory has been that the *Titanic* sank because of a 300-foot gash that cut through the hull and all the watertight holds, dooming the ship to sink. But a naval architect who was on an expedition to uncover some of the mysteries of the *Titanic* has proven that the damage wasn't nearly as extensive as previously believed. In fact, the whole area of impact added up to only about twelve square feet. But it was the location of the damage that sank the unsinkable ship. It was a series of six thin openings across the *Titanic*'s starboard hull, directly over six critical watertight holds.

I'm OK, You're OK

Technically, there never was a shoot-out at the O.K. Corral. You see, the shoot-out actually took place in a vacant lot between Harwood's house and Fly's Lodging House, nearly a quarter of a block away from the O.K. Corral. But it was referred to as the "Shoot-Out at the O.K. Corral" because "Shoot-Out by Fly's Lodging House" wasn't a suitable alternative.

Mark My Word

The second half of *The Adventures of Huckleberry Finn* has been in the Erie County Public Library since the late 1800s, but no one knew what happened to the first half. That is, until 1990 when the first several chapters of the book were literally found in an old trunk in an attic. This trunk belonged to the late James Fraser Gluck, who was a benefactor of the library while he was alive. Evidently, Gluck convinced Twain to send the manuscript to him for the library, decided to take it home to read, and then forgot about it. Gluck died unexpectedly at the age of forty-five in 1897, ten years after the manuscript had been presented to the library. It is assumed that since there was no title page to denote what it was, the manuscript was simply put into a trunk when Gluck's estate was settled.

The shortest war in American history was the
Spanish–American War. It lasted five months,
from April 25 to August 12, 1898.

A Captive Audience

The Alien and Sedition Acts stifled not only newspaper reporters and editors but also some members of Congress. Representative Matthew Lyon of Vermont was sent to jail for four months and fined $1,000 for criticizing President John Adams in a Vermont newspaper. However, his constituents came to his aid, took up a collection to pay his fine, and made him the first congressman to be elected, or reelected in his case, to office while still in jail.

One of the original four parts of the Alien and Sedition Acts enacted on July 6, 1798, The Alien Enemies Act (officially "An Act Respecting Alien Enemies"), authorized the president to apprehend and deport resident aliens if their home countries were at war with the United States. That act was signed into law with no expiration date and it remains in effect today as 50 U.S.C. § 21-24.

It Was the First Second-Rate Burglary

It was a second-rate burglary of a Democrat party office, but it wasn't in Washington, D.C., and it had nothing to do with President Richard Nixon. This break-in took place in 1930 and was ordered by President Herbert Hoover. According to the diary of Glenn Howell, a naval intelligence officer, he and Robert J. Peterkin were ordered by Hoover after "he received a confidential report alleging that the Democrats had accumulated a file of data so damaging that if made public it would destroy both his reputation and his entire Administration." Howell wrote that they had searched the office but found nothing of consequence.

Keep It in the Family

We would like to believe that the United States does not now have, nor ever has had, a royal family or a monarchial system of government. But if you look at the bloodline of certain presidents, you'll see that a number of them have something in common—each other. Take, for example, the thirty-second president of the United States, Franklin Delano Roosevelt (1882–1945). He was a relative of William Howard Taft, Theodore Roosevelt, Benjamin Harrison, Ulysses S. Grant, Zachary Taylor, William Henry Harrison, Martin Van Buren, John Quincy Adams, James Madison, John Adams, and George Washington.

Arrest Mayor McCheese

I guess you could call this a second-rate hamburglary. Richard Nixon, infamous for the second-rate burglary known as the Watergate scandal, was also accused of illegally raising the price of the McDonald's Quarter Pounder from 59 cents to 65 cents. Included in the Articles of Impeachment against Richard Nixon was "21. Bribery, Fraud. Solicited and obtained for the reelection campaign of President Nixon, in June, July and August, 1972, from Ray A. Kroc, Chairman of the Board of McDonald's, Inc., contributions of $200,000, in exchange for permission from the Price Commission, first denied on May 21, 1972, then granted on September 8, 1972, to raise the price of the McDonald's quarterpounder cheeseburger, in violation of article II, section 4 of the Constitution and Section 201, 372, 872 and 1505 of the Criminal Code."

A Real Land Ho

As his crews were on the verge of mutiny, Columbus heard the words he had been praying for—land had been sighted. On October 12, 1492, a lookout named Rodrigo de Triana aboard the *Pinta* saw moonlight reflecting off a distant shore. The lookout was extremely excited, not just for his discovery, but also because he knew Columbus had promised a substantial reward to the first person who sighted land. But Columbus claimed he had seen the reflection the night before and didn't want to excite the crew. So he kept the reward for himself.

***

Thomas Jefferson wrote the Declaration of Independence in just eighteen days.

Going for the Gold

Another American propagandist belief about the 1936 Olympics is that Hitler was outraged because a few black athletes walked away with the majority of medals and left the Aryans hanging their blond heads in shame. A quick, simple look at the record proves this is a false belief. Hitler was quite pleased with his country's endeavors in the games because Germany was awarded the most medals. The Germans won thirty-three Gold, twenty-six Silver, and thirty Bronze for a total of eighty-nine medals. The next biggest winner was the United States with a total of fifty-six medals.

In Name Only

The Hudson River, the Hudson Strait, and Hudson Bay are all named after one man, the navigator and sea explorer Henry Hudson. In 1610, Hudson was financed by a group of English merchants to find the Northwest Passage, connecting the Atlantic to the Pacific Ocean, and thus Europe with the Orient. Hudson thought he was on the right track, but he headed south into what is now James Bay, and his ships became stuck in the ice. After a brutal winter in 1611, his crew was frustrated with Hudson, and they abandoned him, his son, and eleven crew members in a small boat and set them adrift. Hudson was never heard from again. It was not until the 1850s that Sir Robert McClure discovered a route through the Canadian Arctic.

Given the Boot

The Boot Monument located in Saratoga National Historical Park in New York was erected in honor of Benedict Arnold's heroism, his victory in the Battles of Saratoga, and for the injury he sustained to his leg during the battle. The monument is dedicated to "the most brilliant soldier of the Continental army . . . winning for his countrymen the decisive battle of the American Revolution and for himself the rank of Major General." But because he later became a turncoat, the monument does not mention his name and is distinguished as the only war memorial in the United States that does not say whom it commemorates.

Georgia on My Mind

James Oglethorpe originally founded the colony of Georgia in 1732. He was granted a Royal Charter because of his intention to recruit settlers from English debtors prisons, which would theoretically rid England of its so-called undesirable elements. Oglethorpe also outlawed slavery. Another reason for Georgia's significance was that it was a buffer between South Carolina and possible attacks from Spanish Florida and French Louisiana.

Don't Lose Your Head

Savage Indians going on scalping raids is an enduring image in the mythic world of the Old West. But it wasn't the American Indian who first started the scalping tradition—it was the Dutch. During the early 1700s, the Dutch initiated the "scalp bounty": A fee was paid for Indian scalps. And in 1763, Benjamin Franklin pushed the Pennsylvania legislature to approve a bounty on Indian scalps as a way of placating a group of angry frontiersmen (the Paxton Boys) who complained the government wasn't doing enough to protect them.

Oh, Brother!

Randolph Jefferson is a name that most people don't know. But if I mention his more memorable brother Thomas, then everyone knows who he was. Like most people who are compared to Thomas Jefferson, Randolph comes up short in the brains department. But it's possible that Randolph might actually have been somewhat dimwitted. Even one self-effacing Monticello slave named Isaac said this about him: "He was one mighty simple man—used to come out among the black people, play the fiddle and dance half the night; hadn't much more sense than Isaac."

A Symbolic Gesture

Shortly after the Boston Massacre, which of course was named by the Patriots as a propaganda move, Henry Pelham made an engraving of the shootings. Paul Revere "borrowed" the engraving and did one of his own—surprisingly enough, Revere's engraving got to the printers first and is now considered a patriotic icon.

La La Land

Spanish governor Felipe de Neve founded what is now the city of Los Angeles on September 4, 1781, and named it *El Pueblo de Nuestra Señora la Reina de los Ángeles de la Porciúncula* (The Village of Our Lady, the Queen of the Angels of the Little Portion). That's why L.A. is called "The City of Angels."

Born in Vienna, Associate Justice Felix Frankfurter is the only naturalized American ever to serve on the Supreme Court. He was appointed to the Court in 1939 and served until his voluntary retirement in 1962.

Love a Man in Uniform

The Battles of Lexington and Concord spilled the first blood of the American Revolutionary War on April 19, 1775. So when the Second Continental Congress met in Philadelphia on May 10, 1775, they realized that if they acted quickly, they would have the opportunity to bottle up the whole of the British army in Boston. One of the most underrated founding fathers, John Adams, knew that to solidify the ranks of Congress, they would have to win over the delegates of the South. And the solution was already in the room: George Washington, decked out in his old military uniform that he hadn't worn since 1758, was officially given the appointment of commander-in-chief of the Continental Army on June 15, 1775.

Stupid History

Oh, Hale!

On the short list of well-known American patriotic heroes is Nathan Hale, primarily remembered for his famous last words, "I only regret that I have but one life to lose for my country"—which, of course, he probably never said. Frederick MacKensie, a British officer and eyewitness at the time of Hale's death, wrote in his diary that Hale said he "thought it the duty of every good Officer, to obey any orders given him by his Commander-in-Chief." Not as memorable, perhaps, but probably closer to the truth. But who was Nathan Hale? He is considered America's first spy, and on his very first mission, he was captured in possession of maps showing British troop positions. After he confessed, Hale was hanged on September 22, 1776.

Elevating Otis

James Otis (1725–1783) could be considered the lost founding father. He was a Boston lawyer and the man who came up with the battle cry of the American Revolution, "Taxation without representation is Tyranny." It was Otis who first fought against British authority by defending a group of sixty-three Boston merchants against the "writs of assistance," basically Parliament's legal way of sanctioning unwarranted search and seizure. But the reason Otis is swept under the historical carpet is that he went a little wacky (some historians believe he suffered from bipolar disorder or schizophrenia) and became an embarrassment. Otis didn't die on July 4 as did two of the other founding fathers. He went out with more of a bang, having been struck by lightning in May 1783.

✦

Warren G. Harding and John F. Kennedy were the only presidents to have been survived by their fathers.

The Lizard King

During James Madison's second presidential term in 1812, two new political traditions were created. First, no sitting president has lost a reelection campaign during a time of war; and second, Madison's vice president, Elbridge Gerry, a signer of the Declaration of Independence, was the first politician to redistrict, or carve up, a state to give his party an advantage during the next election. His opponents complained the districts weren't symmetrical and had the shapes of slithering salamanders. A new word entered the political lexicon: "gerrymander."

The Real Spirit of St. Louis

In the early 1940s, he warned Jews in America to "shut up" and accused "Jewish-owned media" of trying to push the United States into World War II. Sounds like Adolf Hitler, but it was actually the beloved national hero Charles Lindbergh. Lindbergh, along with Henry Ford, was very conservative. Both were isolationists and held strong anti-Semitic political views. Lindberg visited Germany on several occasions to inspect the Luftwaffe (German air force) and, in 1938, was presented with a medal by Hermann Göring, founder of the Gestapo and Hitler's air minister. Not to be outdone, Henry Ford received a medal from Hitler himself in 1938.

A Rose by Any Other Name

When one thinks of the most notorious traitors in American history two names leap to mind: Benedict Arnold and Tokyo Rose. But there's one major difference between these two—Tokyo Rose never existed. The woman whom most would associate with the personification of Tokyo Rose would be Iva Toguri D'Aquino, who broadcast as "Orphan Ann" on Radio Tokyo (NHK). Other women who might have claimed the moniker were Ruth Hayakawa (who substituted for D'Aquino on weekends), June Suyama ("The Nightingale of Nanking"), or Myrtle Lipton ("Little Margie").

A report from the U.S. Office of War Information published in the *New York Times* in August 1945 announced "There is no Tokyo Rose; the name is strictly a GI invention. . . . Government monitors listening in twenty-four hours a day have never heard the word 'Tokyo Rose.'"

Jack of All Trades

George Washington was more than just the father of our country; he was the father of the first Mammoth Jackass. The existing jack donkeys during Washington's times were short in stature and didn't have the stamina Washington needed. So he imported donkeys from Spain and France. One donkey he received from the Marquis de Lafayette, named "Knight of Malta," was only about four-and-one-half feet tall, and Washington was very disappointed. So Washington bred Knight of Malta to his jennys and the outcome was the first American line of Mammoth Jacks—a breed name including both females and males.

Just Add Sex

Howard W. Smith, a Democratic congressman from Virginia, indicated his intention to keep the 1964 Civil Rights Act bottled up indefinitely and had what he thought was a foolproof plan. To the laughter of his House colleagues, Smith decided to add the word "sex" to the list of "race, color, religion, or national origin" that the bill had been designed to protect. Smith thought it would be the bill's death knell because he assumed nobody would vote to protect equality of the sexes, but he was wrong. The bill not only passed Congress, but it also passed the Senate and was then signed into law by President Lyndon Johnson on July 2, 1964.

Wait a Minute, Man

As Ralph Waldo Emerson put it in commemorating the Battle of Concord, "Here once the embattled farmers stood, And fired the shot heard round the world." Part of the romantic imagery of the American Revolution is that of the Minuteman. Ever ready, the Minuteman was a middle-class, dedicated sharpshooter who could be called out in a minute's time to come to the defense of the new nation. But these beliefs have little foundation in fact. Scholars have shown that most Minutemen came from the ranks of the poor and were paid for their services. They weren't sharpshooters; in fact, they weren't very good shots at all. But they could quickly assemble—mainly because they didn't have jobs and had nothing else to do.

What About the Whites of Their Eyes?

Captain John Parker, who commanded the Lexington militia at the Battle of Lexington on April 19, 1775, was quoted as saying, "Don't fire unless fired upon, but if they mean to have a war, let it begin here." It's doubtful he ever said it. The quote didn't surface until 1858 and was brought to everyone's attention by Parker's grandson, Theodore.

Civil War Union General Lew Wallace (1827–1905) gained his greatest fame not from activities on the battlefield but as the author of the novel Ben Hur: A Tale of the Christ.